The Hidden Wisdom
Within
Numbers

The Hidden Wisdom
Within
Numbers

The Key to
Life Enrichment

A. J. Mackenzie Clay

NOTE: MACKENZIE CLAY now lives in
Merimbula, N.S.W. He is available for
consultation or teaching purposes.
He can be contacted through P.O. Box 633,
Merimbula, 2548. (Tel/Fax 064 957412)

Acknowledgments

To my wife Margaret for all the help and support I have received. To the Universe for giving me a Destiny number 16 and thereby setting in motion the whole of this unending project.

Typesetting, Cover Design and Distributed
by New Dimensions
PO Box 677
Byron Bay, NSW, 2481, Australia.
Ph: 066 85 7034.

Printed by Merino Lithographics, Moorooka, Qld, Australia.

Published by A. J. Mackenzie Clay.

ISBN 0 646 09549 8

Foreword

I guess that I have been *pretty lucky* (55/1) for I believe I have essentially been *on the right road* (72/9) almost from birth. Certainly, when at about the age of fourteen I ceased to go to church, it probably could be suggested, albeit with the benefit of hindsight, that *I slipped into reverse* (105/15) at that point.

Maybe I did, or, on the other hand, maybe I did not, for there has been *no obvious sign* (64/1) of *a turnaround* (48/3) subsequently. So, let me just suggest that perhaps I went at *a slower pace* (49/4), at least for awhile.

Certainly there have been *forward leaps and bounds* (88/16), subsequently though, just about all of these occurred in the last decade or so. I think I have followed *an interesting path* (83/2) and one that became *illumined in light* (88/7).

Clearly *nature's intention* (74/2) was that I would one day become a numerologist, or should I say, a gnothologist - fair enough. Fair enough for I have had *a wonderful life* (70/7) since the eventful month when, three times, bolts of lightning went to ground through me.

Through the pages that follow I have set out the essence of what I believe to be some quite remarkable discoveries I have made in interpreting health by changing names, mine included, into numbers, and from then on deciphering what I believe to be *the interplay of energies* (121/13/31). The same universal energy that was predetermined to strike me in the form of lightning plays out its interactions throughout one's life. *The interplay of energy is all mapped out within the name, illuminating health and attitudinal patterns* (409/49/4).

Being very involved in *herbal medicine* (72/9), I applied my thinking on numbers to the properties of individual herbs and I came up with some interesting findings which I touch upon in the pages to follow.

However, despite my faith in herbal teas, I realised that they could not do one thing. It took me a while to find out what that "thing" was, blocked or *banded energy* (61/7). In a nutshell, more or less *by the time we have reached the age of 20, through our conditioning by society most of us have lost contact with the universal energy source* (555/15/51).

I make no apology therefore for featuring *Reiki energy* (74/2). It is great to be able to glean from one's name all *the life details* (63/9) hidden within, but the question then arises as to how one handles the details and makes them fall into place to be of *personal benefit* (71/8).

The answer lies in learning to use this Reiki energy. Not only does the technique which was rediscovered by Dr Usui re-establish one's contact with *the Source* (42/6), it ostensibly could be said to perhaps *invent one's future* (75/3) because it so gently, so effectively, redirects one back onto the path to *one's spiritual home* (84/3). From my own experience, I do assure you that there is *much excitement* (64/1) as you journey.

As Reiki has so many of *the answers* (42/6), I do refer to it a lot. What I say on *the solar plexus and the subconscious mind* (140/50) is I think important, as it is effectively *the key to unlocking the God concept* (143/17/53). Reiki II involves the use of *the Sei-he-ki symbol* (79/7), which one is told covers *mental healing* (58/5). Personally I think that a far more appropriate description of the symbol's usage is *talking with God* (70/7) for that is what actually takes place. The new student wouldn't probably appreciate the significance, at least for awhile.

I can only urge you to put together what might at first appear to be a random jig-saw of numbers, or numerals. I believe that you will get *a lot of satisfaction* (70/7) from doing just that.

Table of Contents

Chapter 1

The Science of Numbers

To introduce myself and my thinking I have to begin by saying unequivocally that it is *The Universe* (56/2) that has ordained the writing of this book.

Yes, I am using, or should I say adapting, the numerological principles first enunciated by Pythagoras many centuries ago. He applied numbers to names and by doing this achieved interesting insights into personalities. This was the start of what we now name *numerology* (57/3).

I believe, indeed I now know, that the application of numbers need not be confined to just names, but has a far wider application, details of which will unfold as you read on. However, to set the ball rolling I give below the basic key used to obtain the numerological equivalent of all names:

A	B	C	D	E	F	G	H	I
1	2	3	4	5	6	7	8	9
J	K	L	M	N	O	P	Q	R
1	2	3	4	5	6	7	8	9
S	T	U	V	W	X	Y	Z	(Y)*
1	2	3	4	5	6	7	8	9

*Y - as a vowel.

For me *the unfoldment* (58/4) began in November 1981, when I was struck by lightning three times in one month, twice in one night. At that period, it so happens that all I knew about the tarot cards was that card number 16 was known as *The Tower* (42/6), the tower that is struck by lightning. From that I also knew that my Destiny number is number 16. Here you should refer to my details.

So this book is different, very different. Although numbers, or rather numerals, (double, triple, even quadruple numbers) feature in it, it is not at all like normal numerological writings, which like astrological horoscopes are so often featured by the press or on commercial radio.

This book is on *gnothology* (59/5) or *The Science of Numbers* (87/6). I sincerely believe that my thinking which will come through as you read on will prove to be *the key to abundant health* (87/6).

In the ten years that have passed since the lightning strikes, I have been fortunate to uncover some potentially very interesting information which I believe can lead to *a much better understanding of health* (143/17/53), the most precious of everyone's earthly assets.

I am also convinced that locked into *the understanding of a name* (111/12/21) are the clues to *one's spiritual development* (111/12/21). Throughout this treatise you will find "highlighted" what I term as *a divination* (55/1), indeed sometimes whole paragraphs are followed by the numeral equivalent of what has been written.

Systematic working through details will, I am sure, open up for you a *store of knowledge and understanding* (148/13/58) that will surprise you and stimulate you.

Although I mention my own birth date, I concentrate on *the hidden energies within every name* (181/19/91). To highlight the logic behind these numbers, these energies, let me point out that vibration number 18 also covers, besides very many other things, what I term as *the journey to consciousness* (108/18). And vibration number 81 tells that *it is only at the spiritual level that one may readily access energy* (261/27/81).

Life is full of challenges (101/2) and *understanding numbers* (89/8) is *a challenge with a reward* (99/18) that will take you further along *the journey to consciousness* (see above).

As a backdrop to all this one should realize that it is through their education or social conditioning that people are taught to think and solve problems in a certain way, and to only consider certain things possible. This puts a limitation on people's ability to "know" things and strongly affects their beliefs.

Indeed, I personally was a rebel who did not want to be taught what to learn and how to learn it, especially when most of the subjects were incredibly dull. I wanted to do it all my very own way. I had to break out of, what was to me, the bondage of the educational system. I am so glad I achieved this, though, no doubt, I could only have done so with *the assistance of the universe that puts one in the right place at the right time* (279/27).

The human mind (58/4) can be likened to a very complex computer which is only limited in its potential applications by the limitations imposed upon it by the operator, you, your very self. I am sure that there is a great deal of useful information "out there" somewhere, still waiting to be unearthed.

We are all given *a name* (16/7) and the name, whatever it is, just like the name for any given item of food - say, chocolate, banana, whisky, etc. - always conjures up in one's mind a certain inherent energy. It is no different for example with a motor vehicle - such as a Ford, with which I once had a very sorry experience with a new model which had no guts, no energy. As a result, I am most unlikely to purchase another of the same make again.

My research has shown me that *the energy within any given life is hidden within the name* (274/22/94). Indeed, it is

3

possible to discover the interplay of energies within the life at any given point in time, for these energies progressively change with time. I hope I will be forgiven for illustrating my own life (Appendix A).

With a little patience I am sure you can discover the secrets within your own life, or within anyone else's if you wish. It is implicit that interpreting anyone's Kabala must necessarily be done very positively and objectively. Indeed some warning is given on this matter (Appendix B).

The challenge embodied in this book is twofold. Firstly, to the individual understanding these numbers, it can prove to provide both an understanding of *the personality self* (87/6) *as well as the Higher Self, the soul* (104/14). Secondly, to the medical profession, *the understanding of the name highlights the inner activity within the life* (316/37/46), thereby actually showing up what is causing the outer symptoms.

I do not claim to have any medical knowledge, though through herbal medicine over the years, and now with Reiki, I have learnt a lot. As I keep saying, "I may not be right, but ... I am not wrong". In this context it is of interest to note Edward de Bono writing on creativity in his book *"I Am Right, You Are Wrong"* suggesting all *valuable ideas* (42/6) that come about as a result of insight, chance or mistake, must always be presented in scientific literature as if they have come about by a process of stepwise logic. This I believe I have done.

Let us therefore now look at a few words to illustrate, albeit simplistically:

Take the word *health* (851328/27/9), and then look at the words *illness* (9335511/27/9) and *sickness* (19325511/27/9). I suggest that there is relevance in the identical vibration. Certainly there are six letters in the word "health" making it a matter of *integration* (60/6), seven letters in the word "illness" making it a matter of *metabolic rate* (52/7), and eight

4

letters in the word "sickness" making it a matter of *circulation* (53/8). The most important lesson of all comes when we realise that *the liver* (45/9) which is *the Ministry of Planning* (117/27/9) is in the same exact vibration as the above - as is the behaviourial word *anger* (15759/27/9), giving the clue as to how to deal with the problem in whatever form it takes.

Number 3 is the vibration for *self-arousal* (1536 1963113/39/3). We also find in it the words *liquid intake* (398394 95215/57/3). We all know what a lift one gets on a hot day from taking a drink. We all should appreciate the interrelationship of liquid intake to *digestion* (497512965/48/3). All my work shows me that very few people drink enough.

And so we go on to find *water* (51259/22/4) and *urination* (399512965/49/4) have the same vibratory frequency as does the word *elimination* (53949512965/58/4).

Changing style somewhat now, look at the words *water intake* (51259952125/46/1). Those who do not drink enough, are those who dehydrate and suffer *exhaustion* (5681312965/46/1).

Not for one minute do I suggest that my thinking is absolute. I do, however, believe that it provides many indicators of tremendous potential assistance to any practitioner offering health advice. If the medical practitioners don't want to get involved directly in all this, there is now a Wholistic Practitioners Network offering a wide range of health services.

We understand the words sky, sea, sun, sex and God. To each of us they conjure up a certain meaning - but what have they in common? Of course, the answer has to be three letters in each word, number 3 being the number of *self-arousal* (39/3).

Also under number 3 we find *the self* (30/3) and *the name* (30/3). How, therefore, can one understand oneself without understanding one's name? One can't! But, as always, there are other clues - *a man must control his own destiny, so he must be in command of his hidden powers* (300/30), and this clearly eventuates only with an understanding of the name.

So, *understanding the name* (90/9) shows *your hidden powers* (93/3), and this will provide *your destiny* (60/6). We have thus arrived at an algebraic formula which reads 9 = 3 + 6 and, in so doing, we have another of life's answers.

Let me just mention on much the same wavelength, the Reiki II symbol, *Choku Rei* (45/9) which literally interpreted means *all the power of the universe unites in this point* (210/30/3). Here we have, expressed algebraically, 9 = 3 + 6 (the missing number = the number of understanding or integration). So, it becomes essential to understand *the thinking that is behind the energies that are within the name* (270/90/9).

So, now what about myself? I am so thrilled that Providence (57/3) gave me a Destiny number 16, a given name *Mackenzie* (42/6), the vibration that forecasts that *I meet God* (42/6) and a surname *Clay* (14/5), the vibration of *the Higher Self, the soul* (104/14).

Add the two name numbers together, i.e. 42 + 14 = 56 the vibration for *the Universe* (56/2). What more could I have asked of life - nothing more. By the way, I can only comment that it is the Scots who use the favoured surnames as given names.

M	A	C	K	E	N	Z	I	E		C	L	A	Y		Born		9
4	1	3	2	5	5	6	8	9		3	3	1	7			1	4

$$1 \quad 9 \quad 2 \quad 8$$
$$\overline{1 \quad 9 \quad 5 \quad 1}$$
$$1951 = 10/06$$

(Expression number 56)   (Destiny number 16)

From this you will note that there is no number 6 in my name giving me a Karma number 6 - the vibration for *understanding* (60/6). Coupled with this, *the spiritual seal* (69/6), or the number of vowels added together that are in the signature is number 22/4 where we find the divination *the great Divine spirit* (112/13/22/4).

Many divinations have guided my life and will continue to do so. One that has been and is very important to me reads, *maintain a positive outlook on life and expect to live a long time. Your attitude in sickness and in health is extremely important in determining the quality and duration of life* (711/72/81).

The above has been so fundamental to my thinking for so long. As a result I honestly feel that I have been lucky enough to understand *the correlation between the conscious and subconscious minds* (227/29/47) from a very early age, possibly even as early as when my parents moved from Baghdad, where I was born, to Haifa. You should therefore refer to appendix C on this subject. I believe the discipline involved in this understanding is far more effective than any form of affirmations.

So, the important ingredients in the initial understanding of a name are:

- the total energy in the given name
- the total energy in the surname
- add these together to get the total energy in the life,

7

noting that other given names have no relevance, other than in *the signature* (57/3)

- the first and last letters in the given name (M-E=4-5/45)
- the first and last letters in the surname (C-Y=37)
- the first and last letters in the full name (M-Y=47)

Thus from my name, important and active divinations include:

- *the fine line between the spiritual insurance of absolute knowing and the worldly insurance of caution* (411/42/51)
- *the path of gradual spiritual illumination* (176/14/86)
- *all that inherent energy within* (146/11/56)
- *the life force of the universe* (135/18/45)
- *the passing on of knowledge so that other people won't have to go and work it all out again* (343/37/73)
- *good health is no accident, it involves a balance between all aspects of one's life, physical, mental, emotional and spiritual. If any one of these is out of kilter, one's whole growth and development can be affected* (767/47/74)

Although I do not cover the birth date other than my own, there is no reason why, from the mass of detail included in this work, you cannot work yours out. For myself, the major divinations include:

- *The metaphysical wavelength* (113/14/23)
- *The lightning strike on the tower* (151/16/61)

Those who master the details of these numbers will have at their disposal *the knowledge of all life, past, present and future* (182/11/92). *The answers to life* (73/1) are here albeit, perhaps hidden within *the mysticism* (57/3) associated with the need to understand.

The symbols for *Hands-on Healing* (68/14) that were rediscovered by Dr Mikao Usui, now known as the Reiki technique, lay dormant for many years, presumably because people hadn't grown enough spiritually to understand them. I believe that people are now ready to really come to terms with the energies in their life, and they can do this through numbers.

Do not use any knowledge you may gain for self-seeking. Those who are fortunate enough to gain an understanding will have an obligation to use the knowledge to advise others how best they may help themselves. Possession of this knowledge is *the possession of ultimate wisdom* (127/10/19). It is *the knowledge of all life* (99/18).

The Christian races owe their religion to the Jewish culture as surely as the Buddhist races of the East owe theirs to the Hindu culture. The mysticism of Israel supplies the foundation of modern western occultism. Its famous glyph, *The Tree of Life* (71/8), is an excellent and comprehensive meditation symbol.

Although our roots are in tradition, *there is no reason why we should be hidebound by tradition* (245/29/65). *Understanding the Kabala* (85/4) is a growing practice, for each researcher enriches the technique, which then becomes part of *the common heritage* (89/8).

The Kabala is not and must not be taken as a reference to death, for I will never forecast death. The entire 81 year span must be judged and interpreted in reference to *the spirit of the destiny for the life* (173/11/83), which one obtains from the birth date. The whole thinking is based on the fact that by the time one may reach the age of 81, one is either so wise that one doesn't worry about the future, or one is in a state where one doesn't like to think of the future.

Each period of twenty-seven years must likewise be

9

interpreted in the knowledge of the *morphic fields* (89/8) that influence every life. The period of youth is to age 27; the period of power from age 28 to age 54; and the period of wisdom from age 55 to age 81. Each new letter in the name represents nine years of life.

So, using my own name as an illustration:

- **The Youth Triangle** is 4-3-5 with cornerstone/capstone number 43,
- cornerstone/keystone number 45 and keystone/capstone number 53
- **The Power Triangle** is 3-5-5 with cornerstone/capstone number 35,
- cornerstone/keystone number 35 and keystone/capstone number 55
- **The Wisdom Triangle** is 5-5-5 with cornerstone/capstone number 55,
- cornerstone/keystone number 55 and keystone/capstone number 55
- **The Whole Life** is 4-5-5 with cornerstone/capstone number 45,
- cornerstone/keystone number 45 and keystone/capstone number 55.

00	09	18	27	36	45	54	63	72	81
Cornerstone								**Capstone**	
	M	A	C	K	E	N	Z	I	E
	4	1	3	2	5	5	8	9	5
		5	4	5	7	1	4	8	5
			9	9	3	8	5	3	4
				9	3	2	4	8	7
				3	5	6	3	6	
					8	2	9	9	
					1	2	9		
					3	2			
					5	**Keystone**			

The smaller triangles mentioned can be picked out from the above Kabala. From page 11, you notice that number 55 is the most frequently occurring numeral which, albeit perhaps with the benefit of hindsight, highlights the story of my life in the divination that reads, *tapping nature's hidden energies* (145/19/55).

Always read the numbers in consecutive pairs, sideways, reverse sideways, upward slanting and downward slanting. My computer programme actually "adds up" the number of times all the numerals appear in any kabala. With me, number 99 is my most frequently occurring numeral or vibrational frequency. For this an appropriate divination reads, *the subconscious mind in active partnership with the conscious mind* (279/99).

One more trick of the trade worth learning is achieved by:

Youth triangle: add the birth month, number 9 to the first three letters MAC = 4+1+3 to give number 17.

Power triangle: add the day of birth, number 14 to the second three letters KEN = 2+5+5 to give 26 total.

Wisdom triangle: add the year 1928 = 20 to the third three letters ZIE = 8+9+5 to give 42 total.

11

Each of these triangles exert an influence on the life at the appropriate time.

The choice of all names is a serious business and should not be taken lightly. The vibrations connected to names, all have their downside and their upside. This is what life is all about for *we are here in a body to learn, to improve on our past performance in previous lives* (351/36/81).

Self-perfection requires an understanding of both the energies within the name and those missing from the name (469/10/19). In the circumstance it is hardly surprising to find in the same vibration:

- *The law of thought as destiny* (109/19), and
- *The body is the part of the soul that shows* (154/19/64).

So, what about *those energies missing from the name* (159/69)? Well, as you will shortly find out, I believe vibration number 69 is the one most closely connected with longevity - so the logic becomes that it is worth doing something about the missing energies, *the karma* (32/5).

To reiterate - *the choice of an appropriate name for a child is a serious matter, one not to be taken lightly* (362/38/92). Why inflict *a heavy karma* (45/9) on an innocent young baby? I suggest you wouldn't want to endure that yourself. Let me tell you that *it is possible to read from a child's name, the forthcoming divorce or separation of the child's parents* (389/29). Surely, this is a sobering thought.

To illustrate what I am saying take the two words, *the name* (185 5145/30). The missing numbers here are 3,6,7 and 9 = 25 total. Then reflect that *karma is the law of ethical causation, justice, reward and punishment* (241/25/61). Perhaps you will appreciate what I am getting at when I tell you that number 25 is the vibration where one finds *the fine line that exists between self-destruction and self-improvement* (277/25/97).

I do not like the situation where the child has the same given name as one of the parents. Quite simply, if the parent has paid off the karma, then there will be none left for the child to pay off. This is the so called case of *the perfect name* (65/2), and there is, of course, nothing in this world that is perfect. So, there will be problems somewhere down the line.

Where the parent has not paid off the karma, perhaps with illness resulting, one has to expect much the same type of illness in the child which will almost certainly be termed by doctors as *a genetic hereditary factor* (125/17/35) which it will not be. It will be a *karmic hereditary factor* (117/18/27), however.

Every name of any sort has its own karma. Take for instance the word *chocolate* (386363125/37) with missing numbers 4, 7, 8 = 19. Take also the word *sunshine* (13518955/37) with missing numbers 2, 4, 6, 7 = 19. In both cases the karmic accumulation is number 19 where we find a divination which reads *indulge only in moderation, never to excess* (181/19/91).

I sincerely believe that exactly the same thinking is justifiably applicable to illnesses. Take something like *declining eyesight* (94/4), which began to affect me at age 42. Today, over twenty years later, I do not need *reading spectacles* (71/8) for anything. The number missing from the problem (declining eyesight) is number 6 (F, O or X). This is also my own karma, besides being the vibration of *the Divine Law* (60/6), which states that *real healing is spiritual healing* (148/13/58/4).

There is a great deal of work still to be done, and it is time for other minds to cooperate so that we all may benefit. These numbers, these energies, are part of our lives and it is time for us to accept them and to try to fully understand them. The product Coca Cola is so vigorously advertised that the name has almost become symbolic. Numerologically it is a number 26, where the appropriate divination reads *if you are determined to be a winner, this is a large part of being a winner* (296/26). Need I say much more? I believe that a *numerological understanding* (125/17/35), along with the obvious benefits of *the Reiki Hands-on Healing technique* (165/12/75), are the answer that all search so hard for.

At the time of *the fateful lightning strike* (124/16/34), I was, as I still am, heavily involved in herbal medicine. Despite my faith in herbal remedies, I knew there was something still missing. It turned out to be *energy* (40/4), or rather *energy blockages* (70/7). *This affects the metabolic rate* (67/4).

It is just not possible for the human race to live in the modern world without the everyday use of numbers. So, why not get involved, for you will have some fun. Also, do yourself a favour and learn Reiki, and thereby *maximize your energy* (111/12/21).

Chapter 2

Ancient Thinking Revived

Numerologically, I first became really interested in *longevity* (50/5) after my wife, Margaret, mentioned some years ago that she had heard Lord Emmanuel Shinwell interviewed on ABC radio. He used to be heavily involved in British politics quite some time ago. He was to have his one hundredth birthday the following week.

The kabala for the given name, Emmanuel, shows us :

E	M	M	A	N	U	A	L	
5	4	4	1	5	3	5	3	that the cornerstone/
	9	8	5	6	8	8	8	capstone is 53.
		8	4	2	5	7	7	that the keystone/capstone
			3	6	7	3	5	is 53 too.
				9	4	1	8	
					4	5	9	
						9	5	
							5	

It is no coincidence that number 53/8 is the vibration of both *self-healing*, as well as what I term as light magic. So, what is this *light magic*, and how does one self-heal? The answer that will evolve as you read is *Universal energy* (80/8).

Using the given name and the surname Emmanuel Shinwell - 54415353/18955533 = 69 Expression, we find the following divinations:

15

Abounding health	High self-esteem
Real achievement	Openness and appeal
Public exposure	A creative channel

Thus, the only relevant comment is to suggest that each of these attributes is particularly relevant to Lord Shinwell. There are many more possible divinations of course. The final one on the list is of interest because it is a great thing to *have the ability to tap into universal energy* (170/80), and to be a creative channel sharing the energy with others, thus increasing the overall energy in the universe.

A word of appropriate advice for those interested in longevity comes in the divination which reads - *longevous people respond to stress in a calm, serene way. One does not need to repress emotions, but to remain calm and untouched by the chaos all around* (541/55/91). Now just look at the Emmanuel Kabala and notice the triangle under the third and fourth letters. Clearly by age 40 Lord Shinwell had learnt of the benefit of calmness even within the political dog-fighting world.

I have no doubt that there are differing interpretations of the root causes of many health problems. Arthritis, for example, is sometimes referred to as the *nice person's disease* (98/8). Here is another piece of wholistic thinking:

Arthritis: *Feeling unloved. Criticism. Resentment* (212/23/32).

It certainly isn't hard to imagine possible reactions to this interpretation, particularly from *arthritis sufferers* (97/7). We have so much to learn and understand. Just listen to this - *you are holding back on something and this is causing an underactive thymus gland* (311/32/41). To correlate with this one then finds that the *thymus gland governs the heart* (140/50). The logic behind all this improves when one realises that arthritis (50/5) is the very same vibration. To effectively treat any health problem one must locate *the fire within* (82/1). So, we arrive at the answer - *spiritual healing* (82/1).

It is always easy to blame the medics who just don't seem to have the answer. *Pain can become the life enhancing signal it should be, instead of a wholly negative suffering* (374/14/32). My work shows me that the Reiki technique greatly enhances the plight of the arthritic sufferer.

However, all my herbal work shows me that arthritic sufferers just do not drink nearly enough liquids, and there are some very good herb teas for the problem. Circulation (53/8), or rather a lack of it, is definitely involved for *the arthritic condition* (116/17/26) is the same vibration, i.e. number 8.

A while ago I was asked by an experienced naturopath to do a reading on her grand daughter's christian name. The baby was not then twelve months old. I did the reading only to find that *epilepsy* (46/1) was embedded within that particular name. She had diagnosed this and just wanted confirmation. I recommended a course of herbal treatment which has, I am glad to report, been very effective. But all this shows that there is such a lot of information hidden within these names of ours.

The range of enquiries that come forth over a wide range of health problems is fascinating. So, let's now look to epilepsy (46/1) to see if this adds to our understanding of the problem:

Epilepsy: *A sense of persecution. The feeling of a great struggle. A rejection of life. An opportunity for self-violence* (488/38/47).

Could it be said that the above should apply to a young baby - the answer is "no". However, appreciate that my work just highlighted *a possible health dilemma* (92/2). It was not in itself an absolute forecast, only an indicator, and thus presumably a case of *a stitch in time may save nine* (107/17). I recommended a herbal treatment and the baby responded.

To understand the problem in older folk, the divination below is I feel relevant. Once again the solution is for *the epileptic sufferer* (109/19) to learn Reiki.

Sensation exchanges, as opposed to real relationships, can not only ensnare us. This kind of experience always fades rather quickly. It fades because it is often based on a self-alone orientation. In other words, it is not usually of loving someone else outside oneself (1018/19).

So, in leaving this to the reader's own understanding, the only further comment I would make here is in quoting *chemical residue toxicity* (118/19) plus *chemicals from the environment* (136/19), indicating a possible outside influence which causes the behaviourial pattern associated with epilepsy.

Now let us look briefly to chemicals which may be missing from the body. I am convinced that you can actually tell from a person's name what chemicals may be in short supply, and when this will occur in the life. Personally, I have suffered few health diversions, but I did have a spate of bad *leg cramps* (40/4) not that long ago.

From Dr Jensen's excellent work *The Chemistry of Man* I learned that *a silicon shortage can cause leg cramps* (138/12/48). So I investigated silicon and came up with the following divinations, which also happen to be relevant to my own Kabala: - *Silicon aids the transfer of nerve impulses* (177/87).

- *The silicon reserves have been precipitated from the body* (249/69).

- *A silicon deficiency resulting in the cracking of gristle in the knees or other joints* (371/11/38). (I was particularly subject to this).

- *The arms and legs have muscle spasms when silicon*

reserves are low (235/28/55). (My arms didn't have a problem but my legs certainly did).

- *The reserves of silicon are exhausted* (152/62).

A possible exercise you could undertake now would be to go and search my Kabala and find the above double (not treble) digit numerals, for they are all there. It will prove an invaluable lesson in reading your own Kabala. Remember these double numerals don't have to be just read from left to right. They can be read backwards, upwards slanting, and downwards slanting, consecutively.

I must not and do not make any claims with regard to the full understanding of *multiple sclerosis* (74/2). What is of concern to me is the number of people whom I have come across who have, on medical advice, undergone *an operation which is* (has proved to be) *the trigger for the onset of multiple sclerosis* (303/33).

This is a startling statement but it is true, and it does happen, and the results can be devastating. Number 33 appears in the CL of the surname Clay, and none of my relatives have had MS even though there have been quite a few operations performed. However, the point is that a mix of three numerals in the Kabala (74, 31 and 16) is required if MS will be triggered as a result of an operation.

A study of vibration number 74 will tell a lot more about MS:

the muscle reflexes	burden of fear
the woman within	masculine energy
fierce emotion	mental strangulation
fearful of change	don't dwell on the past

As with any number vibration the list of divinations both negative and positive is extensive. Also I am certainly not suggesting that everyone with a number 74 in their kabala will become *a multiple sclerosis sufferer* (119/29). We are

19

trying to get a new understanding about containing MS. In this context the best pointer to the prevention of multiple sclerosis is almost certainly *Reiki energy* (74/2).

As a Reiki Master it would be inconsistent if I wasn't a believer in the energy, for it is a gentle technique and it unquestionably is one of the best ways to balance fierce emotions. It also helps *resolving conflicts* (87/6) between *the competing masculine and feminine energies that are in every individual's personality* (201/21). This is achieved so naturally and without taking sides in any *internal conflict* (76/4) that may be happening.

The male and female aspects of every individual have to become balanced or brought into harmony sooner or later (435/48/75). *Different selves take over at different times and, the self that is on top at any particular time can act as a dictator, doing what it likes. And it can compromise all the others, so that what it does the others pay for* (767/74).

God forbid, for I am certainly not trying to suggest that MS sufferers need *psychological counselling* (116/17/26). To repeat - I believe that Reiki can achieve *the necessary act of balancing* (108/18). I suggest that it really should be learnt by any MS sufferer once diagnosis has verified the condition.

There is another clue to understanding the condition. *Blockages in the throat chakra are a resistance to the feeling of emotion. Always have faith in what you are doing* (434/74). *Through the throat chakra one communicates and forms judgements of others* (288/18/27). This is the vibration associated with *anger* (27/9), which may explain the root cause of the MS problem.

But now I must turn to another medical problem that interests me - *bowel cancer* (47/2). This vibration is, of course, number 74 written the other way around, and recall that I have said that you may read all consecutively paired numbers in any direction.

A doctor was brought in to see me by his wife. He had one operation for bowel cancer but the problem was reappearing. I asked him if he was *shy* (18/9) and he said "no", though his wife said "yes". I explained, too, that *whenever there is shyness there is a thyroid dysbalance* (236/29/56).

A *thyroid dysbalance* (82/1) is the same vibration as *spiritual healing* (82/1). Herein lies the real answer also as with MS. To see what stage we are at, let's look at two vibrations - number 82/1 and number 55/1.

82/1		**55/1**	
Spiritual healing (P)		lasting health (P)	
My inner turmoil (N)		my unaware soul (N)	
My false brain signals (N)		insecurity (N)	
Energy harmony (P)		peace of mind (P)	

(P - positive and N - negative traits)

My message and my advice is simple. Have all illnesses looked at from more than just one point of view, for you could be very surprised at what you discover.

Medical testing had evidently shown the doctor with the bowel cancer to have *a normal thyroid* (76/4), though wholistically this clearly was not so. In this context I can only comment on when I was asked about two children in the same family who had been put on *insulin* (35/8) for *diabetes* (29/2). After computer examination of both names, I indicated to the parents that I felt that there was no diabetes, to be told that a naturopath had also come to the same conclusion. So, again, two opinions are better than one, and you may be very much better off for having taken the trouble to get the second opinion.

Of course, I was flattered when asked to do a name reading for one of the leading consultants in the holistic advisory field. After a few polite preliminaries, I turned and said to her, "S, your problem is that you are *sexually repressed*". (85/4).

"Gosh", she replied, adding with a sigh, "You know you are absolutely right and you are the first person I have ever admitted it to". The relief of having allowed the problem to come out and into the open was obvious and more than half the battle in solving the problem.

Perchance, under the very same vibration, one finds *the conception vessel* (85/4), and also, *hate is an expression of vulnerability. We tend to mask it with defensiveness and blame so that we won't have to admit how vulnerable we really feel. It is important to express feelings of hurt directly and, if possible, in a non-blaming way* (886/76/85).

So, it was that the problem became identified which provided *the opportunity to express the associated feelings* (211/22/31). This produced the stimulus to do something about solving the problem, which has I am sure happened. This lady became convinced that her husband was *playing around* (67/4). I don't think this was the case. Any form of hate is *a negative thymus gland attribute* (121/13/31). This makes it a number 4, and the same vibration as *the human mind* (58/4), as well as the several number 85/4 divinations referred to above.

Descending down the body, we find both *my feet* (31/4) and *a bunion* (31/4). Nowhere have I ever come across an explanation of what a bunion is, so let's see if I can provide one, for although obviously often associated with *ill-fitting shoes* (76/4), I think there could well be an *electromagnetic toxicity* (121/13/31) involved.

The impact on the body of electromagnetism (171/18/81) - from power lines, computers, microwaves, etc. - is far wider than most people would accept. I well remember talking to a lady whose husband's name was Alan and saying to her - Alan happened to suffer from *haemorrhoids* (71/8) - "Alan's problem has to be associated with *electromagnetism*" (71/8).

22

To this she responded, "Ever since marrying him, I have been saying we must sell this house". The home was very near overhead powerlines. So, now let's therefore briefly look at the name Alan.

A	L	A	N
1	3	1	5
	4	4	6
	8	1	
	9		

And what do we find? The first three numbers on the top line of the Kabala read 131/41, the number vibration for the divination which happens to read, *a harmful electromagnetic effect*. And then the AN reads 15, the divination for virtually the same, i.e. *harmful electromagnetism* (105/15). If you are wondering why you can't see the number 71 associated with haemorrhoids, it is because it appeared in the surname, which obviously I musn't mention.

Whenever *psoriasis* (44/8) occurs it is invariably associated with *electromagnetic damage* (91/1). Is there any wonder that the same vibration applies to *the brain chemistry* (91/1)?

The neck contains many structures, including the blood vessels carrying blood between the heart and the brain, separate passages for air to go to the lungs and for food to reach the stomach, and various glands such as the thyroid (821/11/83).

So it was that when my spiritual path found me investigating energy at Mahikari, each energy treatment focussed on the neck first - *the store of tension* (83/2).

To illustrate this very real point a nineteen year old student called Elena came to see me. Her expression number was number 53. So, isn't it interesting to find these two divinations in this vibration:

frustration (53/8)   *my stiff neck (53/8)*

Elena has potentially exactly the same kind of future as Emmanuel Shinwell. However until she gets over the antagonism she has towards her family set-up, where she happens to be the youngest, she has problems.

As one surely limits the range of physical movement by rigidifying and armouring one's musculature, so one also limits one's mental powers with fears, intellectual conflicts and contractive beliefs (848/38/83). The Karma on the name is number 36 - 45 minus 5+3+1, or, missing numbers 2, 4, 6, 7, 8, 9 = 36 total, where the relevant divination reads *turmoil* (36/9).

Appreciate this - *the neck represents the ability to be flexible, to see the other side of the question, and to see the other person's viewpoint. A neck problem usually means that one is being stubborn about one's concept of a situation* (860/50).

We musn't leave *the neck* (30/3) without referring to *the shoulders* (55/1) where we find the divination, *rounded shoulders represent a person with a past problem* (230/50). Elena indeed had a past (relationship) problem. Of course, *a past problem* (48/3) only becomes *a present problem* (71/8) to the extent that one continues to hold onto it.

It sounds incredible perhaps, but there are a number of given names where *a potentially dramatic forecast* (119/29) is embedded within. It is therefore surprising to see their continued usage. One such name is:

T	I	F	F	A	N	Y
2	9	6	6	1	5	9
	2	6	3	7	6	5
		8	1	9	4	2
		8	1	5	6	
			9	6	2	
			6	8		
			5			

Here we find a cornerstone/capstone 29 and a divination which reads, *my parents either divorced or one of them died when I was young* (281/11/29). In itself this is not a prediction, but more a statement of reality for the life when it looks backwards to ponder events or happenings.

I personally feel that parents, perhaps even irresponsibly, tend to *play around with names* (86/5) for their forthcoming child. Sometimes the parents make life hard for themselves as well as the child - *a learning lesson* (66/3) indeed.

I guess choosing a name is a bit of a lottery really, but does it need to be? It doesn't, because now there really is a lot of knowledge behind *the meaning of names* (79/7). I can only say that I was so lucky, for my parents quite definitely told me that they picked *Mackenzie* (42/6) from *The London Daily Telegraph's* Birth Notices. I commend their choice!

But let's return to Tiffany, and indeed to Trevor, about which my interpretations also apply, for another divination reads, *a life in need of a shoulder to cry on - a danger in marrying too soon* (274/22/94). Then notice number 22 in the first line that slants down to the right. It is exactly the same with Trevor, and the practical interpretation of number 22 is literally that *you must not marry until after age twenty-three* (211/22/31). For the want of any other description, possibly this might be called *a premonition* (59/5).

Have a look at the 66 in the first line of the Kabala with the 3 below and between. Here we have *both* two 36's and two 63's, for always the numbers are read in pairs in any direction but they must always be consecutive numbers. The literal interpretation of both numerals is respectively *the woman* (36/9) and *the male within* (63/9), which shows up the inherent dilemma of conflicting energies within both of these names and, therefore, lives.

Of course everything may turn out for the best. This is always a possibility though not an implied reality. I have touched on the potential conflict when dealing with MS and, yes, the name Tiffany does contain the number 74. The name Trevor does not. Interestingly, MS is more common in females than in males. It is perhaps more appropriate that *the female energy* (79/7) should come out on top, for it is *the intuitive energy* (103/13). However, *the gut feeling* (67/13) that I have suggests that it will be the other way round. The conflict arises because *masculine energy tends to be physical* (147/12/57) with the risk of babies coming along, which sooner or later will prove to be a millstone around the life.

Balanced internal energy (103/13) will prove to be *the wheel of good fortune,* (112/13/22) whilst *an energy imbalance* (79/7) could very well produce *vascular heart disease* (79/7), *cancer of the rectum* (79/7), *Petit Mal epilepsy* (79/7), and so on. The point is that *banked-up energy will sooner or later find its own path out, if it isn't released naturally* (349/79).

Readers of my earlier book *The Numbers of Health* will appreciate that part of my devotion to the study of *the science of numbers* (87/6) continues to be to try to unravel how it was that my sister, Marjorie, managed to die at the ridiculously young age of 50. She was indeed the family's *blue-eyed baby* (48/3).

Sure, alas, my parents would not give their consent to her marriage with the original man of her choice. Alas, I was overseas at the time and wasn't in any position to influence them from a distance. Such things do happen.

M	A	R	J	O	R	I	E
4	1	9	1	6	9	9	5
	5	1	1	7	6	9	5
	6	2	8	4	6	5	
	8	1	3	1	2		
	9	4	4	3			
	4	8	7				
	3	6					
	9						

When I last saw her, she informed me that she would soon be dead from cancer - quite frightening, but so true as it turned out. Look at the two 46's in the second and third line which govern the period from age 36 to age 54. Here, the relevant divination reads, *literally eating your body with cancerous growths because of being unable to forgive the past* (586/46/55). Now, find the consecutive numbers 2-1-7, with number 2 in the second line slanting to the left, number 1 in the third line, and number 7 in the fourth line similarly slanting. Then note the divination which reads, *the point of total variance with parents and a calamity* (217/28/37).

Notice the three 48's where one finds *the black hole* (48/3), for this is really what poor Marjorie became entombed within. It was all so tragic of course. Incidentally, my parents insisted on calling her *Daw* (10/1) after the nursery rhyme "See-saw Marjorie Daw" (72/9). Here (10/1) is the vibration of *the gastro-intestinal tract* (100/10/1) which almost certainly accounts for the start of my sister's cancer.

I am not trying to apportion blame either to my sister or to my parents. It is all a matter of these numerals or the interplay of energies. Use of the nickname only actually did harm, for it was used constantly from a very early age. A brief look at the kabala shows:

D	A	W
4	1	5
	5	6
	2	

It is quite frightening to note *cancer* (26/8) as well as *a time of crisis* (65/2) in the same line. Then one finds *the brain's signals* (65/2) which is probably very true. Use of Reiki would have been excellent then, but, it was not to be, for I did not know of it at that point.

The name *Doreen* (34/7). Anyone whose name starts with the letter D is always *a thoroughly reliable person* (132/15/42), although sometimes one does find *a lazy tendency* (60/6). The expression number should involve the individual in *the social scene* (57/3), particularly when there is a Karma 21/3 which you get by counting the numbers missing from the name (1,2,3,7,8). With six letters in the name, one can expect *harmony* (42/6). With the overriding letters D-N = 4-5/45, one can expect *common sense* (45/9).

The three number 5's give the name a lot of *power* (32/5). David Phillips in his *Secrets of the Inner Self* suggests that *such power is too difficult for most people to handle* (274/22/94). I think he is right. Without a number 3 in the name, there will be *a tendency to shyness* (77/5). There will also be *intense drive and feeling* (113/14/23/5).

The interrelationship of these number vibrations continues to fascinate me. As I have said, you can read these numerals backwards or forwards. For example, *a hard heart* (48/3) and *no heart connection* (84/3). Next, we find *the heart rate* (57/3), and *a heart condition* (75/3). And, going a bit further, there is *my barricades* (56/2), and *my depression* (65/2). Coincidental - no; logical - yes.

I am aware of a case where someone was advised to have *investigative surgery,* (106/7) only then to be put on *antidepressant drugs* (81/9). I cannot see that this got anywhere near dealing with *the deep-seated problem* (90/9), or as I sometimes term it, *the problem within* (89/8). There is always an explanation for the manifestation of *a health problem* (64/1), which in this case was, I believe, entirely due to *barricades erected in self-defence* (139/49), because she knew that the church would not allow her to marry one particular divorced person. As a result, depression ensued and, yes, she had number 56/65 or number 65/56 in her kabala. Having personally got over the medical condition know as *tinnitus* (36/9) or *ringing-in-the-ears* (96/6) without medical assistance or advice, I am going to show you how I tackled the problem. So, below is the kabala for tinnitus along with that for arthritis, simply because I believe the same logic applies in getting on top of them and thus overcoming the unwanted condition. It is the same old story, namely, what is in a name. The answer is predictable and is a great deal of useful information.

```
T   I   N   N   I   T   U   S
2   9   5   5   9   2   3   1
  2   5   1   5   2   5   4
    7   6   6   7   7   9
      4   3   4   5   7
        7   7   9   3
          5   7   3
            3   1
              4
```

```
A   R   T   H   R   I   T   I   S
1   9   2   8   9   9   2   9   1
  1   2   1   8   9   2   2   1
    3   3   9   8   2   4   3
      6   3   8   1   6   7
        9   2   9   7   4
          2   2   7   2
            4   9   9
              4   9
                4
```

Now this is what one learns from the kabala for tinnitus:

1. The cornerstone/capstone is number 21/3 which tells us the problem lies in *the blood supply* (66/3).

2. The cornerstone/keystone number 24/6 focuses on the *kidneys* (33/6).

3. The keystone/capstone number 41/5 directs attention to *the spleen* (41/5).

4. The most frequently occurring number in the kabala is number 75 which represents *an energy blockage* (75/3). Remember that we can reverse the numbers. We then find *the master gland* (57/3). The way I conquered the problem was to use *a magnetic collar* (62/8) at night, which greatly improved *the blood circulation* (89/8). Then I used *crystal energy* (68/5) on my pituitary because I believed that *the vagus nerve* (59/5) was playing up and affecting *the sinuses and the upper lip* (115/16/25). Focused on *the pituitary* (66/3) and *the upper lip* (65/2), the results were remarkable. However the trump card in the *self-treatment* (50/5) was the Reiki. Everyone reacts slightly differently and you must appreciate this. If you have the problem your numbers will tell you where to concentrate.

Arthritis comes up so often, so perhaps I may be forgiven for mentioning it more than once. There are nine letters in the name which focuses it on *the liver* (45/9). Then *we learn that an adequate liquid intake is essential for proper liver function* (270/90/9). Notice that there are eleven number 9's in the kabala, so we are getting near the solution. Then appreciate the advice which reads, *mastering pain simply by relating and concentrating on calm and ease* (270/90/9). Give this approach a go.

Six number 99's tells one to *control the emotions* (99/9), as well as what I term, and here I am talking for the *arthritic sufferer* (111/13/21), *my hostility and anger* (99/9) and *imprisoned energy* (99/9). Tackling health problems this way provides *an understanding and a new approach* (134/17/44) to solve so many problems. Is there any wonder that vibration number 44 covers *The Light* (44/8)?

Then appreciate the significance of the divination which reads, *mastering pain simply by relaxing and concentrating on calm and ease* (270/90/9). We are beginning to get near to the solution, for in a full kabala there are forty-five numerals, and in the one for arthritis there are eleven number 9's. There are also four number 8's which is the number of *the emotions* (53/8).

Proceeding further we find six number 99's, the vibration which says both *control the emotions* and *my hostility and anger,* as well as *imprisoned energy.* Here is a sure reference to the potential for the part Reiki can play in overcoming the complaint, especially when we realize that number 42, of which there are several in the kabala, refers to the *low voltage.*

Tackling health problems this way provides an understanding and a new approach to solving these common complaints. I am sure of one thing, namely this approach is well worth investigating.

A word of caution for the Richards and Ronalds of this world, for both their names are overridden by R-d = 9-4/94. I have found *a heart attack* (37/1) to be a common factor, which is perhaps not surprising considering the vibration number 94 also contains *uncontrolled energy* (94/4). This is not a matter of clairvoyance, I assure you.

However, do note - *heart attack: energy which is not used turns back upon itself and attacks its own body. Men who neglect to use their feminine drive (their anima) are especially vulnerable, because their feminine drive is the creator of the heart connection* (931/94). In this context do note *the feminine drive* (94/4).

Sympathy must go to teachers who discover they have a child with *development problems* (87/6). Just think about the divination that reads, *my early problems, the signal for my parents marriage break-up* (256/22/76). Now reflect on the names Burt, Brett and Benedict, where the overriding letters in each case are B-t - 2-2/22. Of course, I know of instances where there has been *no break-up of the parental marriage* (145/19/55). On the other hand, I know of cases where just such *a break-up* (30/3) has occurred.

The area of concern is probably more with the child, who is likely to be *self-contained, self-sufficient and isolated from others* (472/22/49). We are talking about *a person's happiness* (79/7), as well as *the need to reach out* (79/7). I am not advocating that teachers should become marriage counsellors, but they should at least be able to recognize what is happening, at the very least through an understanding of the child's name.

I am not in the business of *divorce* (40/4), nor do I ever want to be in it. However, I can well recall a client coming in to see me where I said to her, "You are an interesting person. Four men are going to get close to you in your life". She replied, "Don't worry, I have been married and divorced three times. I want you to pick the fourth person."

She was under 45 and her name was not Lynnette, which is the name I am now going to illustrate:

L	Y	N	N	E	T	T	E
3	9	5	5	5	2	2	5
	3	5	1	1	7	4	7
		8	6	2	8	2	2
			5	8	1	1	4
				4	9	2	5
					4	2	7
						6	9
							6

Notice the three number 55's, the first one coming on-stream at age 27, the second between age 27 and 36, and the third between age 36 and 45. This is reading the kabala with the lines angled to the right. You can take your pick, for number 55 reads both *sexually active* (55/1), as well as *I remarry* (55/1).

Notice the two number 56's, the first of which comes on stream at age 27, and the second between age 27 and 36. Here one finds the hidden wisdom saying *late marriage* (56/2), as well as *a sudden romance* (56/2).

But, possibly most importantly, and going back to number 55, we find *the awakening* (55/1). This about sums it all up for the figure 5 is shaped to start on the physical plane, then it goes upwards, where it hooks into the emotional plane before reaching skyward to the spiritual plane.

The name Lynnette is a Motivation 19, (add the vowels, 9+5+5) and a Psyche 12. Now, number 19 represents *the wavelength of spirituality* (136/19), as well as *a life that is spiritually inclined* (136/19). I guess therefore that it is reasonable to conclude that number 55 as "the awakening" is thus referring to a spiritually-based awakening. Confirmation of this comes from the psyche number which tells of *uncovering the real self* (102/12).

One should always try to interpret the kabala objectively. For example notice the four number 27's. These come on stream at age 18 and go right through to age 81, though they peak at age 45 (vertically down from the letter E). From this we can learn:

- *a full circle of retained energy around the genitals* (216/27). Knowing this perhaps highlights the problems!
- *awakening is a process that has many levels. It goes on unfolding in its own time* (297/27). Knowing this perhaps aids in understanding the problems.

There is yet another, a hidden gem of surely welcome news, and this reads, *after success in working up a business, I am finally ready for marriage* (279/27). Overriding the name is L-e = 3-5/35 which provides quite an influence over the life, e.g. *to fully appreciate light, to first experience and understand darkness* (341/35/71). So one thing is for sure, and that is that there will be *interesting developments* (110/20) in the life of anyone with the name Lynnette. Having said this, of course one must assume that every person of this name will have a different birth date which in each case will create its own special influence.

Historically the term *marriage* (45/9) was connoted to develop *the concept of protection* (112/13/22/4) - man and woman forming *a partnership* (64/1) based on providing protection for each other. Perhaps it is because no *real protection* (72/9) evolved between the partners, that they *divorce* (40/4).

Success in marriage is thus a matter of *complementing or competing energies* (174/12/84) along with what amounts to a *determination to succeed* (99/18/9), albeit possibly somewhat *idealistically* (62/8). Today the emphasis has, I suggest, shifted away from marriage or *a physical partnership* (105/6) to one of *a spiritual partnership* (108/9).

So, to return to the terms *I remarry* (55/1) and *the awakening* (55/1) as they occur in the name Lynette, I suggest that number 55 has thus the ability to signal the change from the physical partnership to a spiritual partnership.

I want to talk briefly about the term *forgive and forget* (91). I guess it could be said to apply to many marriages. I believe that exactly the same principles that I have been enunciating can be applied here. Notice that there are 16 letters in the saying, then reflect that number 16 is the vibration which tells us *united we conquer, divided we fall* (142/16) - surely, very pertinent advice. And, number 16 goes on to mention *the need to train one's emotional nature* (151/16) - also a very pertinent reflection. Certainly too, it has a relevant warning signal too - *emotionally overreactive* (115/16), and *so emotionally insensitive* (115/16).

There surely are so many hidden truisms within the energy levels embodied in just about every life situation. Then we learn of *the learning process* (91/1) - so apt; of *grace and pressure* (91/1) - an excellent attribute to acquire; and of *a personal recycling* (91/1) - possibly not sought but almost surely necessary, indeed essential. Then, on the downside, it mentions what I call *my emotional prison* (91/1), and *my inevitable downfall* (91/1). Number 91 comes on stream in Lynette's life at age 18 and lasts right through to age 54.

To make the perspective whole, I quote from *What's Wrong with You* by Dorothy Hall who says, *"the trigger for the onset of diabetes may include a secondary cause as well as the primary one of emotional distress which registers in the liver resulting in a new allergic response at the bottom end of the vagus nerve near the pancreas"* (928/91).

The only possible comment to all this is that a chemist would know precisely what happens when one combines the *latent energy* (73/1) in, say, sulphuric acid with, say, a piece of iron. In just the same way it is up to each of us to interpret *the possible energy response* (128/11/38) both attitudinally and bodily in each and every human situation. These numbers are indeed the tools to use to do just this.

Nothing has occurred to change my belief that *the interaction of numbers represents energy in motion* (247/67/22/4), either mathematically or numerologically. It is therefore no coincidence that the word *energy* (40/4), as well as what I term *a magic wand* (40/4), are in the same vibration. Also, please appreciate that *God is energy* (67/4).

In pursuing this line of thinking, surely we are *getting near to the answers* (107/17)! Perhaps this becomes more relevant when one realizes that number 17 also reads:

- *the secret of quantum healing* (116/17/26), and
- *cancer: a possible path to enlightenment* (152/17/62).

Returning to vibration number 4, I particularly like the divination *The Pearl* (40/4). Why? Because one finds other gems that are hidden within the vibration, and I am positive that there are many others that await discovery. Examples include *Man's heritage of cosmic knowledge and spiritual wisdom* (220/40), and, *the ripeness of the body - the nourishment and attachment* (220/40), and, *each one of us has a universal spark which is capable of being contacted directly, activated, expanded, and used in our daily lives to promote healing, wholeness, energy balancing, to prevent disorders, and to maintain a state of positive wellness, and for our own personal journey of transforming and awakening* (1210/31/4).

The numbers that do not come up in the kabala are the 10's, 20's, 30's, etc. They may however appear in the motivation, psyche and expression numbers, with reference to a person's name, or they do occur in birth dates in some form e.g. (19)90, (19)80, (19)70 and so on. Here, *the energy factor* (83/2) with clear significance is the last of the two pairs of numbers.

So, what may we perhaps expect from those born in 1990 - on the positive side, we find:

- *confidence and assurance,*
- *literary excellence,*
- *intellectual capability,*
- *psychic discovery,*
- *healthy self-assertion*
- *self-starting activity,*
- *a winner this time, and*
- *the key to a fuller life.*

This is particularly interesting in view of the divination which reads, *rebirth is the light at the end of the tunnel* (180/90). Naturally, as with all number vibrations, there are negative divinations for number 90, but I don't intend to focus on these other than to mention that they all would fall under the banner of *consciousness raising* (90). In other words, if you fail to maximize on *life's wonderful opportunities* (141/15/51), it will have been because of a negative attitude. Indeed, number 90 is the vibration of many opportunities.

But, really, isn't all life *a matter of balance* (56/2) or, put another way, *the recognition of opportunities* (164/11/74)?

When someone fairly close to you gets a problem like *cancer of the prostate* (86/14/5), inevitably you become concerned. So, I feel it appropriate to say something on the subject. It so happens that vibration number 14 covers *enlargement of the prostate gland* (131/14/41/5).

To me, this is no coincidence, especially when the same vibration also talks of *balanced energy in the bladder meridian* (167/14/77/5), which is fine provided the energy is balanced. One learns *the predominant emotional states affecting the energy balance in the bladder meridian are restlessness, impatience and frustration* (500/50/5).

36

Restlessness (39/3) is in the same vibration as *the third chakra* (39/3), and one also learns that *the third chakra is located in the solar plexus. It manifests in the pancreas and governs the action of the liver, stomach, gallbladder and certain aspects of the nervous system* (669/39/3).

So, once again, we are getting clues which can help in understanding the problem which centres around *the bladder function* (82/10/1). Then we also find *the thyroid gland* (82/10/1). The problem is that the medics are faced with a situation - *prostate cancer* (59/5) - and they have to deal with it, often urgently. I appreciate that it is inappropriate to go back and try to find out where the problem may have started, possibly, indeed probably, many years ago. However, really, we are concerned to create a situation where it is possible to identify *potential problems* (71/8) in others, long before these become *real problems* (55/1).

You see, the next clue comes in both *cancer of the prostate gland* (106/16) and *thyroid gland function* (106/16), thus focussing attention on the interrelationship of the two. I can only add that I believe that the thyroid is far more fundamentally linked with a number of physical problems than is generally realized.

You should refer to the definition for *restless* (27/9) and, in doing so, appreciate that number 98 covers what I term as *the cancer personality*, as well as some wonderful attributes which include:

high-thought analysis	*a commitment to excellence*
experiencing life	*interesting activity*
strength of character	*cutting through obstacles*

Speaking of the body, number 99 does however have *pancreatic dysfunction* under its umbrella. And, having said this, we have surely come just about full circle in looking at the problem with different spectacles. One notes *the pancreas gland* (67/4), and in the kabala in this case there were two number 67's. Looking around a little further note *a thyroid energy deficiency* (146/11/56). This particular 3-digit number, as well as number 56 on its own, was in the kabala and right on target for this person's present age. *The pancreas is the master gland controlling all other glands* (230/50) - here we have the solution. Certainly, all that I have written amounts to being wise with the benefit of hindsight and after the event has occurred. What I am suggesting are pointers only. Surely, any pointer that directs the wholistic practitioner's attention to where the solution or understanding of a health problem may lie, just has to be worth following through to help and assist in the recovery process.

As one would expect, *improved blood flow* (89/8) identifies that *the problem is circulatory* (118/19/28). This very same 3 digit number also covers *a channel for cosmic energy* (118/19/28), highlighting *energy circulation* (93/3). This is significant: *the prostate* (48/3) and *the blood supply* (66/3).

Time and again, my numbers work indicated that when the letters C, L and U (each of which equal a number 3) are missing, there will be *a thyroid problem* (84/3). This applied with this person. It can be confirmed when a pendulum is held over either the signature or the name.

Now, let us have a look at two very similar, yet quite different names:

The cornerstone/keystone for Lawrence is number 37 and applies to age 45. An appropriate divination might

L	A	W	R	E	N	C	E
3	1	5	9	5	5	3	5
4	6	5	5	1	8	8	
1	2	1	6	9	7		
3	3	4	6	7			
6	7	1	4				
4	8	5					
3	4						
7							

L	A	U	R	E	N	C	E
3	1	3	9	5	5	3	5
	4	4	3	5	1	8	8
	8	7	8	6	9	7	
	6	6	5	6	7		
	3	2	2	4			
	5	4	6				
	2	1					
	3						

well read, *whenever there is a tendency to repress one's sexuality, one immediately becomes improperly grounded. Should this happen the likely casualty to follow will be either one's body-mind or one's spirituality* (847/37/82).

The cornerstone/keystone for Laurence is number 33 and applies to age 45. An appropriate divination might well read, *instead of trying to control and force your mind, you should lead it lovingly to the ecstasy of the Self. If you turn the mind to the supremely blissful Self, it will want to run there as fast as it can, but if you suddenly try to make it peaceful by force or austerities, it will become more and more agitated and turn against you* (1293/33).

The keystone/capstone for Lawrence is number 75 which applies from age 46 to age 81. An appropriate divination might well read, *the unhappy person feels that the fault always lies with someone else. There is always the feeling that if only the powers that be, right down to one's parents had given more* (723/75/93).

The keystone/capstone for Laurence is number 35 which applies from age 46 to age 81. An appropriate divination might well read, *because anger is caused by what you perceive to be unfair, it is a moral emotion and you will be extremely hesitant to let go of that righteous feeling. You will have the nearly irresistible urge to defend and justify your anger, sometimes even with religious zeal. So, overcoming this will require an act of great willpower* (1295/35).

The cornerstone/ capstone for both Lawrence and Laurence is number 35 and applies right up to age 81. It is worth noting that where a key number repeats itself, as with Laurence, nature is saying in effect, you are not going to make a success early on so you will be given a second chance. An appropriate divination reads, *disease may be largely a spiritual issue. Healing may be attained through a regaining of inner harmony and peace of mind* (485/35/44).

Let's turn now to the word *energy* (40/4). In effect, energy represents *the power of doing work* (112/22/4). Perhaps we must have a look at some of the things vibration number 22/4 can tell us:

- *the subconscious mind in active control of the conscious mind* (238/22/4)
- *the conscious in partnership with the subconscious or God* (265/22/4)
- *the source of great contentment hidden within you* (211/22/4)
- *the awareness of a divinity* (112/22/4)
- *life is made of energy and energy is in perpetual motion* (247/22/4)
- *touching the source is how the mind creates its patterns of intelligence* (292/22/4)
- *illumination by The Light provides the energy that can burn out disease* (292/22/4)
- *the ability to successfully tap into natures hidden energies* (238/22/4)
- *a symbol is an image with an inner hidden meaning* (202/22/4)

There is always more to every vibration, but I must move on because reference to energy is certainly not confined to a single vibration. So, look now at the divination which reads, *energy cannot move in a situation where two parts of yourself, the tyrant* (the subconscious mind) *and the rebel* (the conscious mind), *are doing battle and you are not dropping into your intuition for guidance* (667/64).

It so happens that *energy can only be acquired by finding and understanding nature's hidden secrets* (334/37/64). Any individual can of course achieve this and the answers are I honestly believe within this book, this discourse on numbers and on energy. *Turn on your light and go forth and teach others* (198/18).

The cornerstone/capstone for the word energy is number 59 (see below). As this is the vibration of *free choice* (59/5), it is entirely up to any individual to be either aware of energy, or to disregard energy thereby making the life much harder. In the same vibration one finds *the master mind* (59/5) and of *illumination* (59/5). Under 667/37/64 (see above) mention was made of dropping into the intuition. In the standard noughts and crosses layout *intuition* (50/5) is so conveniently situated in square number 5, and midway between squares number 6 and number 4. Thus it literally is a case of dropping into the intuition.

```
3  6  9
2  5  8
1  4  7
```

Most of us experience intuition as something that comes and goes, bringing useful information or spiritual insights, but in a random, mysterious way. Once one learns to recognize how one's intuition communicates, one can then apply it to practical problem-solving, understanding relationships, finding spiritual guidance, and answering one's own questions (1436/59).

```
E  N  E  R  G  Y
5  5  5  9  7  9
   1  1  5  7  7
      2  6  3  5
         8  9  8
            8  8
               7
```

The cornerstone/keystone of the word energy is number 57. Here there are some lovely, yet so simple divinations which read, *you* achieve a sense of balancing by becoming at one with nature (237/21/57), a man of vision (57/3), faith in God (57/3). Now, using the keystone/capstone Number 79 one finds *a meeting with God* (79/7), and *the way to reach God* (79/7). I am sure I could go on with the same analogy on the most frequently occurring numbers within the kabala, but perhaps you might like to try this for yourself, for you might be surprised at what you come up with. My suitably produced computer programme will lighten the task for you.

The problem of *overweight* (60/6) is one that affects many folk. Just by looking at the word itself one notices:

- The word is ten letters long. This is termed Key number 10/1. This is the same vibration as for cell regeneration (82/10/1). It is not surprising therefore to find some useful comment. Firstly, *the male all too often has solid energy impeded around the solar plexus, making him emotionally prone* (406/10/1). This points to learning Reiki as *an energy release* (75/3). Secondly, and applying to all, we learn that *cell regeneration is achievable by imaging the spirals of the body's cells turning in the opposite direction* (460/10/1). In Reiki II one learns about *the spiral symbol* (70/7) known as *Choku rei* (45/9). This is tremendously significant in implementing *quantum healing* (64/10/1).

- The word overweight is overridden by O-T = 6-2/62/8. This tells us something, for it is here that we find the term *the body image* (62/8). Putting this slightly differently, *if you expect to be overweight your subconscious mind will oblige you by providing the emotions necessary to complement your conscious thinking* (620/80/8).

The self-image (56/2) is far more important than most people realise, and it is no coincidence that in this vibration one finds also *real healing* (56/2), as well as *a beautiful body* (56/2). I am not referring to being a top model, but just simply to the fact that *beauty is in the eye of the beholder* (147/12/57). Here it is no accident that this vibration includes *a sense of health* (57/3), *my wellbeing* (57/3), and *my happiness* (57/3). So, now, *go look into the mirror and realise how beautiful you are* (262/28/82/10/1), and you will see instantly how significant *a good image* (50/5) is. It is your *free choice* (59/5). *Beauty is everywhere* (96/6) - the mountains, the seaside, the rivers and lakes, the flowers, shrubs and trees, and, of course, in *the self* (30/3).

A feeling of inner contentment and peace (161/17/71) is appropriate in view of what I have been saying. In the same vibration one finds, *a perfect body - an image of health - healing powers - inward looking - internal power - the Divine spark - positive wellness.* What more can one ask? Alternatively, there is - *hardness of heart - an unrealized soul - a chronic illness - the negative ego.* It really is up to you to choose your path and to keep on it.

Still under the same vibration, the wisdom goes on with *the way a person perceives the world affects his or her own physiological processes* (341/35/71). Next we find such a valid truism, *the only thing required for hearing your inner guide is your willingness* (341/35/71).

More and more doctors are beginning to tell that *successful patients learn to motivate their own healing, and the most successful go much farther than that, for they have found the secret of quantum healing* (773/53/71). It is within your powers to achieve this.

At this juncture it is appropriate perhaps to mention that Reiki II teaches what is termed *mental healing* (58/4).

Personally I prefer to call the discipline *accessing white light* (93/3), or *the healing potential* (93/3), or *the God that is within* (93/3).

I want to briefly turn to the word cancer (26/8). Notice that the word is a Key number 6, as it has six letters in it. This makes the word one of *harmony* (42/6). Next notice that the word is overridden by the letters C-r = 3-3/33. The karma for the word is number 27 (number 2, 4, 6, 7 and 8).

So, what can we synthesise from all this:

- Number 26 tells us of *low thymus glandular activity* (116/17/26), and to *reflect that anger both poisons the mind and sours the stomach* (233/26/53). It goes on to say, *the past is the past. You must let it go and move on to the present* (251/26/71).

- Number 33 tells us that *when we constantly suppress and distrust our intuitive, looking instead for authority, validation and approval from others, we give our personal power away. This leads to feelings of helplessness, emptiness and a sense of being a victim, eventually to anger and rage, and, if these feelings are suppressed, to depression and deadness* (1284/33).

- Number 27 tells us *God is the spirit that breathes life into all living organisms and leaves them with a degree of freedom to explore the possibilities of reaching their potential* (47/27/72). It also goes on to define *a signpost: the resolving of inner turmoil or conflicts leads to healing* (297/27).

It so happens that *disease* (26/8) is in the same vibration as cancer. Now, the definition for disease directs our attention to vibration number 44/8. This also covers *the fire* - the cancer itself - as well as *The Light* - the cure for cancer, and, of course, much more. Then it gets our thinking nearer the solution by saying, *an individual's thought projections can easily close off the energy supply to the thymus gland, the controller of the heart* (494/44).

I am convinced that far more health problems owe their start to *electromagnetic radiation* (115/16/25) than is generally realised. It was no coincidence that within a space of just three weeks two Barrys crossed my path, and both had cancer. So it is appropriate to look at the kabala for the name.

B	A	R	R	Y
2	1	9	9	9
3	1	9	9	
4	1	9		
5	1			
6				

I have a particular divination which reads, *a hot spot of electro-magnetic energy* (121/13/31), which has always proved to be an effective aid in diagnosing health. In the case of the first Barry, he lived underneath powerlines and he too actually commented to his wife the previous week, "I want to sell our house". The second fellow owned an engineering firm that used many electric-powered machines.

Thus, in this kabala one notices straight away the two number 31's. Then notice the 1111 slanting down to the right. Here an extremely significant divination reads, *a serious health condition* (111/12/21). Notice the 23 that starts the downward slope in the kabala and harken the divination that reads, *electromagnetic distortion of the brain's signals* (203/23).

So, bit by bit, one zooms in on more clues. Oh, for sure, you might suggest that these are somewhat fragmentary - just remember that the study of *electromagnetic disturbance* (113/14/23) is in its infancy, at least as far as health is concerned.

It is certainly worth commenting on the six number 19's and the two divinations which read respectively, *disordered brain signals* (109/19) and *a life-threatening illness* (109/19).

We thus reach the position where there are a good few pointers and, in doing so, we fall back on the staid and tried position which reads, *one only pointer is not enough, two pointers are better but three will make it a certainty* (361/37/91).

Recall the fact that these numbers may be read in any direction, provided that they are read consecutively, and realise that number 19 thus also reads number 91. So, is it a coincidence that number 91 also reads, *the brain chemistry?* I think not. So what did I do for these two Barrys? The answer is Reiki. *Reiki is an excellent way to alter the brain chemistry, and thus the brain's signals* (312/33/42). Please notice the 312 that appears at the start of the kabala.

Personally, I like the name Barry, which hinges around the vibration of *light* (29), B-y = 2-9/29. I do not discount the name providing only that it is fully understood. No life is ever written-off almost as it starts. Perhaps it isn't visibly obvious, but there is always *light at the end of the tunnel* (111/12/21). It becomes a question of when, and the kabala shows it to be any time from age 27 to age 36. The only problem is that some people always seem to run *behind schedule* (65/2).

Any form of *holding-back* (50) in any area of life, be it work, hobbies, sex, etc., almost inevitably produces *a state of creative inertia* (102/12/3). The instances that come up of couples who share a double bed but never touch is astounding. Let it act as a warning that *one's sexuality* (56/2) is in the same vibration as *self-paralysis* (56/2), for this is perhaps what it really amounts to.

From the same vibration we learn that *on the emotional level it is our resistance to feeling that causes us pain. If because we are afraid of a certain feeling we suppress it, we will experience emotional pain. If we allow ourselves to feel it and accept it fully, it becomes an intense sensation though not a painful one. If a sensation isn't really dangerous, you can relax into it and the pain will diminish and dissolve* (1424/56).

In the vibration for *self-inflicted pain* (83/2), we also find that *there is no better way to reach out and touch your partner than by becoming as sensual as possible* (353/38/83).

A brief word now on *touch* (22/4). Firstly, a note of caution - *in need of "a shoulder to cry on" - a danger in marrying too soon* (274/22/94). Next something that is so true for so many - *it sometimes appears as if we have been in school for our entire lives, receiving an education that teaches us the exact opposite of the way the universe actually functions* (652/22/67).

Next, do harken this, *each experience has a seed of wisdom in it for you. What challenged you last year probably seems easy to handle now. What challenges you today will seem easy to handle next month, and so on. Your ease comes from the experience of going through the doubt and uncertainty, or the fear and anxiety that happens when a challenge comes up which seems bigger than your resources. So, when you are facing a new situation which requires a greater resource of knowledge or compassion, you can handle it by drawing in extra resources of light* (2056/22).

Finally, regard the vibration as:

- *The way to deeper and deeper levels of knowing and feeling* (238/22/58)
- *The conscious mind in partnership with the subconscious or God* (265/22/85)
- *You are not given a desire by the Infinite Creator without also being given the ability to accomplish that desire* (472/22/49).

There is much that can be written on these numbers, and in due course no doubt will be written. This work would be incomplete in itself without mention of number 87/6, which ranks with me as perhaps being the most important vibration, for it has within it:

The key to abundant health	The point of mastery
A life without limits	A new level of knowing
The top of the spiral	A new phase of growth
God is a man's best friend	All ideas come from God
Dog is a man's best friend	The desire for love

"Dwell Ye on these things" (96/6).

Chapter 3

From the Past to an Enriched Future

In a higher frequency of light, unresolved conflicts from the past will get stirred up (372/12/39). Old fears come to the surface to be handled. Any anger, resentment, guilt, or jealousy still hanging around from the past can be changed. *Everyone deserves the blessing of a powerful purposeful life* (260/80). So let the still small voice from within keep telling you this, for it can become a great support for your expansion, and a powerful one, too.

We understand the future and the past psychologically in terms of *desire* (33/6), which relates to the future, and *memory* (37/1), which relates to the past.

By consciously changing memories of the past, you free the energy that was holding each negative memory together (480/30). Then you can use this free energy for *fulfilling your highest possible future* (181/19/91). The process activates your imagination so that a new future can unfold like a rich tapestry.

You can set up the future you want when you know how to change your past (264/21/84). All anyone has of a past experience is a memory. Who is to say that you have not already changed what actually happened with your selective memory - leaving out certain parts, emphasising and exaggerating others?

By connecting a bridge of Light into a memory you can illuminate the negative memory pattern and dissolve it

(443/47/83). Next, you can replace it with a new experience which feeds the subconscious mind with powerful positive memories.

When you create a memory of being wise and loving, your life becomes more flexible and open (376/16/34). When you change a memory, your life immediately shifts to accommodate this new reality and your sense of self becomes stronger. What used to seem like the only choice can open to new choices.

Now that so much light can come into one's life, one can see a wiser choice. *Once one can acknowledge that one did the best one could, one is ready to release the memory and build a new one in its place* (447/42/87).

The past is the past. It is past. You must let it go and move on to the present (251/26/71).

One cannot change destiny already made; it is the field of action provided by one's thoughts. *The future may be changed by submitting to the destiny already provided and changing one's thinking* (407/47).

Always remember that "the watched pot never boils", so do not become too attached to a desire (318/39/48). *Every thought is like a piece of the future when it is created, a piece of the present when it is experienced, and a piece of the past after it is gone* (603/63). As long as each impulse is healthy, the future is not unknown - it will flow naturally from the present, moment by moment.

Even though a person truly wants to change, a sense of loss may be felt when an old and familiar habit is erased from the life (454/49/94).

The energy involved in rut-breaking will give rise to an ever-changing sequence of images with yet more subtle meanings (503/53).

The spirit always tends towards expansiveness, depth,

greater energy and aliveness (318/39/48). The form
(ego/personality) always tends towards what it perceives to be
safety, security, and the status quo, which is usually a
deadening experience (105/15). If you are able to observe
yourself without rationalization or judgements, you will begin
to notice that *when you trust yourself and follow your energy
fully you feel better* (284/14/23).

*A personality has no molecules in it, being composed only of
memories and psychological tendencies, yet these are more
permanent than the cells being affected in an allergic reaction*
(722/74/92).

You don't have to be perfect to be a channel for the universe
- *be yourself, be honest and spontaneous* (133/16/43), and the
more freely will the creative force flow through you. As it
does, it cleans out *the remnants and pieces of old blockages*
(142/16/52). *What comes out may sometimes be unpleasant
and uncomfortable, but the energy moving through you will
feel great. The more you do this, the clearer your channel gets,
so that what comes through is an increasingly perfect
expression of the universe* (1800/90).

*Once you have experienced and released blocked emotions
from the past, a greater flow of energy and vitality will enrich
your life. If you are in touch with your feelings as they arise,
they can continue to move through and your channel will
remain clear* (1039/13).

You may tenaciously clutch onto the status quo (158/14/68) -
that which you are used to - and think you want the comfort
and security of old habits, even though you have outgrown
your need for them. Eventually, these *outgrown habits may
start to pinch* (133/16/43). (926/98)

*People really do want to change their old worn-out habits.
Yet there is at least an initial resistance to overcome in almost
everyone* (510/60).

Repatterning The Brain (107/17) - Living in the Now Rather Than in the Past.

Only by changing the idea of yourself can you rewire your brain in ways to allow you to perceive the reality around, to which, for all intents and purposes, you may be presently blind. Reiki helps in the reconnection of the wiring in ways that will give you different sight, different sense.   (1184/23)

A seed will explode in your rewired brain, not a physical explosion, *an energy explosion* (94/4). Then the reality you perceive will be a reflection of that rewiring. So, close your eyes and relax, while taking a deep breath. If you are experiencing feelings, feel them. Should you be feeling fear feel it. Love it all and live it, for you are now all you need to be in the present, to understand anything you wish to be at any other moment in the future.   (1761/87)

Fully realize that *your present* (59/5) is not the result of *your past* (36/9). By effectively reprogramming the brain, the connection with your past is broken. Well done - now take another deep breath.   (735/15/78)

You will begin to experience things in the physical reality which will show you that you no longer have the need for what is called "memory". For you will know everything you need to know in the present - in any situation you create, you will know what you need to know. The need for you to "learn" in the way you have been so used to will disappear, and *you will begin to learn by experience in the moment* (220/40). Perhaps you were so entrenched in habitual patterns from the past - this has now gone for good.   (2016/27)

Your experience of *the present* (49/4) will be the result of what you think it is of "now". If you think your present is the result of your past, that's the effect you are creating. But you are creating the effect *now in the present* (79/7). Now you will only experience the manifestations in your life, the feelings in your life, and the belief systems, which go toward supporting the new being that you are at this moment. Now you will be creating the past from the present, and not the other way around. (1922/14)

You will achieve *a higher degree of energy expression* (188/17/98). You could feel the acceleration of this energy in various ways - fever, flushes, shoulder pain, anxiety, even migraines. This will only be a disorientation until you get used to the new level of energy. There could even be some literal disillusionment, whilst you redefine your physical reality as an extension of the new you. (1552/67)

In a sense, whilst *old habits* (36/9) are dissolving within you, any disorientation that you experience is because there isn't so much solid structure for you to continue to hold onto. It is as though you are floating in the centre of your being, making up your mind as to what the new structure will be like. Give yourself a little time to settle down, and you will acknowledge that the change that has come about through learning the Reiki technique has surely been worthwhile.
(1804/94)

Remember always that anything which may be termed *a blockage* (30/3) is not actually a block, unless you choose to treat it like one. A block is usually information you really need to know, but which comes in an unexpected package. You may not recognize it on the surface, but that doesn't mean it doesn't belong in your life. So, unwrap it and thereby find out what information it can bring you. Then hold tight to that which may still be useful. (1564/61)

In *the transformation* (80/8), you finally realize that *you are the creator of your reality* (156/12/66). The physical reality is your expression and your projection; it is actually made of you. When you grasp this, you will see yourself as the dimension of experience, of which you previously thought you were only a component. Each person will experience themself becoming *the whole dimension* (90/9), and will realize that they have absorbed within all other consciousness they previously experienced. (2015/26)

Each being will have a different dimension of experience resulting from different frequencies of existence - a different density, a higher density or more accelerated frequency, a less material frequency and so on. (914/95)

The processes that make up consciousness must not be thought of as being a product of physicality, for *physicality is itself a product of consciousness* (193/13). As the brain cannot see itself objectively, consciousness cannot be understood in a mental way even though it is the product of the interaction of *electrical activity* (82/1). (1189/28)

As you begin to live more in the now, *in the present* (63/9), not so much worrying about *the future* (43/7) - the more you live *in the now* (45/9), the less you experience the idea of time itself. You will move as you feel you need to move, and you will automatically be where you need to be when you need to be. You will simply know what you need to know when you need to know it. You will be living *in the moment* (55/1) and you will fear nothing, and you will be consciously aware of everything in your life as your creation. (1963/19)

Within any given life you can create many so-called purposes, as there are many ways to obtain fulfilment through which you express who you are. Not one of these represent your purpose - they are your chosen method for expressing the purpose of your life. *Your fundamental purpose is to be the person you have designed yourself to be* (309/39). Always be the fullest you can be, because you will never be this you again. (1605/75)

You, as the you you are, only have one life to live. You have got one shot only at being this you (361/37/91). Even though the soul you are may experience many lifetimes, each of those lifetimes is unique, and a distinct expression of the overall soul you are. Since you have never been this you before, and will never be this you again, *the fundamental reason for this life is to fully be the you you choose to be* (285/15/24). (1527/69)

Many of you go through life looking for a specific thing that would seem to be the purpose of your life, but create difficulty in finding that, because you don't recognize that it is up to you to decide what that thing is. The idea is that the choice was made by the Higher Self, and that (the fact that you are present in the physical reality) is generally referred to as predestination. (1520/62)

There may be some generalized ideas that are also representative of *the overall predetermined reality* (157/13/67), decided upon by you when you were *the Higher Self* (76/13) in a non-physical realm, before you became physically born. The specifics of how you go about living the life, and the themes you find yourself exploring within it, are completely up to your determination as a physiological being. It is all up to you and your free will. You are the representative and the emissary in the foreign land of physical reality. (2048/23)

The stage has now been reached where every being can be called *a God-thought* (54/9) - one of the ways God has of thinking of Itself, of expressing Itself, of experiencing Itself. *You have been God manifested as a physical individual* (205/25), with an individual personality and identity. This is one of the ways *the Infinite* (65/2) experiences Itself. (1313/44)

The Excitement (61/7) - what does it tell?

The things that come with excitement are the answers, are the signals, are the signposts - for that is what excitement is.

Excitement is tapping you squarely on the shoulder and saying "this is what you want to be doing right now". The reason it excites you is because it is aligned with the idea of who you are. (1177/25)

Excitement then tells you, because it is who you are. If you act on it with trust and conviction, it will be the one thing that can be the most effortless thing you ever do - because it is who you are. When you are being yourself, of course it will be effortless. *The only time you have to struggle and experience pain is when you are trying to be someone you are not* (424/46/64). (1377/45)

You must realize that excitement, in whatever form it may take, is the thing that, if you do it, will support you in *the most abundant way* (64/1), to allow you to keep doing it in a more expanded, ever spiralling way. Thus, *you will automatically be able to attract the opportunities to allow you to do the thing that excites you most* (394/34). (1199/29)

Excitement is the thread that leads to all other excitement, as long as you are acting on the things that excite you most with integrity. (512/53/62)

Excitement tells you that it is, of course, you. It goes on to tell you that because it is you, it will be *a new creation* (56/2). And then it tells you that because it is you and will be an effortless creation, you will be able to attract the abundance you need in whatever form you need it. Remember that abundance is more than just money, and it will express itself along the path of least resistance rather like a lightning flash. (1478/56)

Excitement - what you feel to be the physical sensation, or the knowledge, the knowingness of yourself that is translated as excitement - is your physical translation of the vibratory energy that represents the path you chose to be in this life. (941/95)

Experiencing Abundance (104/14)

Abundance is the ability to do what you need and want to do when you want to do it (280/10).

What do you care if *abundance* (29/2) can come in a number of different ways as long as you still have the ability to do what you want, when you want to do it? Abundance is of course a general idea, whereas money is a tool. Being abundant does not have to be attached to the idea of being morally bankrupt. (1016/17)

If you judge someone appearing to have too much money, you are changing your vibration to the same level. If you judge, you become that vibration. Then you can't be where you want to be. (703/73)

One soon notices certain individuals with *obvious physical abundance* (101/11), but who appear *morally or spiritually bankrupt* (137/11/47). This may cause you, without consciously realizing it, to automatically equate abundance with *moral bankruptcy* (66/3). Do not be judgemental, because of course being abundant does not have to be attached to the idea of being morally bankrupt. (1311/42)

If someone has sufficient *symbols of abundance* (67/4) in his life, he will be able to accomplish what excites him as smoothly, effortlessly and easily as anyone else, for the universe will always support you by supplying you automatically with whatever opportunities represent your ability to continue to be who you are, if you are willing to act that way with integrity (57/3). (1434/57)

Personal Beliefs (68/5) - The Reality

If you happen to believe that you have to struggle in order to make a living, perhaps you are one who believes that nothing which does not contain struggle will work for you.

Then the universe will support you in that idea totally. If that is the way you want it, you will get all the situations attached to that belief. So, be warned! (1213/34)

Acknowledge any feelings that you may have of doubt or even fear, because if you don't you cannot transform what you do not own. And, when you can acknowledge having chosen a negative scenario, the situation quickly gets back under your control. (893/83)

It is always up to you to decide how best to blend in with your environment, though *your overall mission* (91/1), more often than not, has been decided by *the free will of the higher self* (148/13/58). (708/78)

Life situations will be given to you automatically by the universe to show you exactly what your beliefs are. They are not to prove you are stuck in anything, nor to prove that you have failed in something, but to show you beyond any shadow of a doubt *the reality that what you believe in is true, it eventuates* (218/29/38). So, if you don't prefer it, then change your beliefs. (1368/45)

Talking about trust brings to mind doubt. *Doubt is a total, absolute, unshakeable, unswerving conviction in a negative reality* (297/27). Always remember this and don't say you haven't been told. *If you are totally behind some idea or belief, the universe will always back you up* (313/34/43). (923/95)

Perhaps you have the feeling that something you are doing isn't being done quite right - fair enough. However, when you acknowledge that whatever you are doing, you are doing it because you believe it to be alright, then paradoxically you will probably change. As soon as you allow where you are to be alright, you will be able to get where you want to be much faster. (1436/59)

Whether you are living *in the past* (40/4), or living *in the future* (57/3), nothing you need to work with can find you as in the present, for *you are not at home* (70/7). So, where do you put your trust - obviously in something you prefer right now.

(926/26)

You are on *the threshold of credibility* (137/11/47). In exploring that threshold, ask yourself what you are truly willing to believe is possible for you. Listen to your answer, which will indicate where the threshold of credibility is. Once the threshold of credibility is squarely within you in the present, you will experience the life you desire.

(1480/58).

Always reflect that as long as your threshold is out there somewhere in the future, no matter how close it is to you, it is not in you and you won't experience it (609/69).

Ask yourself a number of pertinent questions, and truly see if you can picture or feel what you have in mind. Understand that when you are doing what truly represents the vibration of your reality, for, when you are in sync with the path you chose to be, everything is already on that path and in the format it needs to be. It will all fall into place as it needs to fall to let you continue being the person you chose to be. You will automatically, effortlessly, and coincidentally, attract into your life all the tools necessary to allow all details to be taken care of. (2160/36)

You don't get into a reality before you have created the inner belief (282/12/21). *You always get in physical reality only what you already believe to be the most likely reality you'll get* (409/49). (691/61)

When you truly believe with your whole heart and soul *this is really me* (69/6), you will generate *the energy within* (93/3), and your outer reality will have absolutely no choice but to reflect that inner feeling, that inner knowledge. *You must tune in the wanted frequency first or you will listen to the wrong programme* (363/39/93). (1260/36)

To become excited does not imply jumping up and down every single moment. You must realize that the idea of a peaceful knowledge, an absolute certainty, can represent excitement concerning the vibes that allow you to know that you are in sync with the path you choose to be. You need a very steady conviction, a balanced knowledge, a certainty. You do not have to be running around all the time. (1445/59)

Right Now - In the Present You'll See What You Want To See (211/22/31).

If you truly allow yourself to understand that what you are doing *right now* (51/6) is the most important thing of all right now, then you will start looking at it that way. Your attitude will change and you will start realizing that *you are where you are for a reason* (143/17/53). Then you will start allowing yourself to get out of a particular moment what you really need to. Previously, such a moment would have seemed to contain nothing for you that would generate excitement.

(1780/88)

Feelings are a reaction to a belief (136/19/46) and consequently secondary to beliefs. *Beliefs are the primary interface of reality, not feelings* (258/24/78). *First you believe something is true, then you get the feeling, followed by the reinforcing thoughts* (431/44/71) which themselves may reinforce the beliefs, causing you to regenerate more of the same feelings. If you believe you are competent that's fine, and, if you believe you are incompetent, you simply chose that belief, but you don't have to. (1866/93)

You can't expect to see "out", if you are not prepared to see "in". This is actually why so many people need *reading spectacles* (71/8), often whilst still in the prime of their life. The seeds you plant within yourself are what you see growing in the garden around you. If you do not like the flowers you see growing, *plant something different* (116/17/26) and then *something new will grow* (109/19/10). *The inner is the outer* (98/17). If the outer is not the way you prefer it to be, change the inner and the outer will follow.   (1922/14)

If you find yourself using phraseology that indicates you are attempting to convince yourself, then you do not believe it naturally. Talking of reading spectacles, when you say *I want to see* (41/5), this contains an element of unfulfilled expectation. Whereas, if you say *I intend to and will see* (88/16), this has *all the hallmarks of a definite belief* (142/16/52), providing only that you do not waiver.   (1429/52)

If you constantly treat your delivery system (your thoughts) as if it is malfunctioning, then you are not listening to it. You are thinking something is wrong within you, and therefore that's the belief that gets reinforced. If you say to yourself *what will go wrong* (81/9) often enough, *something going wrong* (113/14/23) will be what your reality reflects back to you.   (1458/54)

Only when you acknowledge your own format for the delivery of messages to yourself, exactly and completely the way it comes to you, do you create the conscious freedom to transform that delivery system (those thoughts) into a way you prefer it to come.   (1168/25)

Oh, Those Habits (59/5)

Maybe you have *old habits* (36/9) that seem difficult to break. If you believe in the idea of habits, turn your thinking away from *the difficulty in changing* (128/11/38), to new *very positive habits* (93/3) where you are in control of everything. You wouldn't knowingly drive a car that was *out of control* (57/3), so why ever let your life drive you up a *dead-end street* (57/3)?   (1138/49)

Always be prepared to remove *excessive expectations* (91/1), for events don't have to manifest exactly as your ego or your habits think they should. Allow events to manifest along *the path of least resistance* (98/8), and cease any tendency to fight yourself.   (892/82)

The Whole of Life Involves Change (143/17/53).

Whenever *the potential for change* (105/15) creates anxiety within you, you should try and come to terms with the fact that *anxiety and excitement are the same energy* (174/12/84). If you understand that and start acting as if you believe it, you will feel the energy as excitement and not anxiety. You will continue to feel the energy, but in a way that is indicative of how you now look at it. Know that it represents the discovery of something new, and that you are on the threshold of more information and awareness (244/28/64).   (1903/13)

As you will never go faster than you are ready for, you needn't worry, for you will always be able to handle the energy. If something were to come to you that you were not really able to handle there would be no point - and the universe does not do pointless things.   (1011/12)

Do what excites you most, in the way it excites you most to do it with integrity, and you will always be being of service. *Anxiety* (37/1) is the same energy as *excitement* (44/8), with *judgement* (36/9) placed upon it.   (732/12/75)

Get out into the world doing what you most love doing, knowing that the world will shape itself to what you need (435/48/75), for there is no conflict as it will do the same for everyone. No one loses because you are winning. *You will win because there is enough for everyone* (217/28/37).   (1024/16)

If sometimes you feel you do not have what you need, all you need to do is to acknowledge that you are willing to have it. Then act to the best of your ability on what you can do. Use your imagination and let the rest take care of itself.

(844/34/88)

There is always an appropriate audience for everything that truly needs to be said, and you will find that audience. *Anyone wishing to be on a particular stage will find their audience* (277/25/97). There is never an actor born without an audience.

(921/93)

As you choose the life, the path, the attitudes and the habits that are more representative of *peace and creativity* (84/3), you will crystallize the events in your life to allow only certain types of opportunities and certain types of situations to occur.

It will become more and more difficult for you to choose anything that is not representative of what you really desire, of what you prefer. Your life will then truly be in sync.

(1690/79)

There is no reason to hesitate or delay doing what you really love to do. *There is no reason to hold onto situations and relationships that are not representative of you* (383/23/32). Allow them to change gracefully with integrity and love ... Feel it all, know it, desire it, be it and act it.

(1047/12)

As you act out what is important to you, what you prefer, with more and more of this energy, this vibration, this frequency being radiated out generally, everyone will become more sensitized, more sensitive to each other. You will then be able to key off each other more clearly without the negative confusions of certain *habitual customs* (49/4), which now bind you and keep you from your heart's desire. (1591/61)

Allow yourself to feel that *change is the true constant in creation* (152/17/62). The true stable foundation of existence is constant change (54/9) - so that it does not stagnate. *Change is forever perpetuating* (145/19/55), never is it over. We are all together, *God creating itself anew* (100/10), ever changing and always existing. (1055/11)

You are creating furrows in the ground in farming the richness of your past experience (392/32). Negative though some of it may seem to be, know that it will form *a very rich compost* (86/5). All that has been negative or wasted will allow fertility and new growth to occur, once you place it in the proper place behind you, beneath you, and then grow from it. Let *the light from your future self* (147/12/57) draw you upwards from *that rich soil of experience* (132/15/42), for it is a rich experience. (1864/91)

For every single thing that you truly want to do, that is truly representative of you, there will always be a place and a time in which it can be done. You would not exist if that were not so. (710/80)

Creation is not one-sided but always complete. For every desire, for every true self-wish, for every soul urge (or motivation), there is always the opportunity to manifest that wish in the reality that you are in right now (888/78/87)

Motivation or soul urge (100/10) should be thought of as *paying-off the karma associated with the higher self* (219/39). (401/41)

Gratitude (42/6)

One of the essential preconditions of gratitude is that there must be *a sense of need* (49/4). When there is no sense of need, there is no sense of gratitude. *As soon as we start taking things for granted, we lose the ability to be thankful* (279/99). Always remember to give thanks to the universe for its bounty. (1076/14)

It is perhaps too much to suggest that we be grateful for our difficulties while we are in the midst of them. But it is not too much to suggest that we refuse to let them destroy our gratitude completely. We need to recognize that *any problem or trouble we experience is a sign of our need* (247/22/67). The universe is awakening our sensitivities and sympathies.

(1359/45)

In allowing suffering, the Universe is always looking toward some good. Never are our troubles punishment for what happened yesterday; they are responses designed to help something better to happen tomorrow. *When our whole attention is focussed on reacting to the past, or even trying to prevent things from going wrong, events are not likely to turn out well* (608/68). But the moment we catch a glimpse of what might be, the moment we start working for some *real improvement* (78/6), everything changes. The people we are dealing with start to get the message that we believe in them, that we believe *things can improve* (85/4). (2411/62)

The Universe believes in us whether we believe in ourselves or not - if not, why were we allowed to incarnate (439/79)? The Universe knows that we are capable of deeper love and understanding. After all, *the Creator sent us here* (94/4) and we are part of Him, and because of this, like Him, we too can grow. We tend to see our troubles negatively as we do not share this belief. It is just as well that the Universe gives us nothing but simple things to do. (1600/70)

We have no real idea of how much we have to be grateful for. We are sustained in life moment by moment, by processes we don't understand, let alone control. So it takes troubles or problems to remind us of our need. (771151/78)

The Spiritual Goal - The Higher Self (152/17/62)

The Higher Self (76/4) is exactly what the words imply - *the best possible elements of your own being* (170/80), *the most reassuring aspect of your own inner strength* (222/24/42), *your personal expression of the Divine in you* (209/29). It is your

65

channel to the enormous resources of the human potential.
(1074/12)

When connected to the Higher Self you are aligned with *your spiritual heart centre* (123/15/33) and in touch with the *universal source of strength* (133/16/43). You are functioning *in the light* (58/4) when motivated to proceed from that centre to make decisions to act and to change. (993/93)

To be cut off or to ignore *the heart centre* (69/6) is to intensify conflict, ultimately causing one to be much out of alignment with oneself or out of ease with *the God that is within* (93/3), soon to become dis-eased. (766/46/73)

Whenever you feel *real stress and deep conflict, or extreme suffering* (207/27), go within yourself into meditation space and ask *what is it that you have forgotten about yourself*, your own inner strengths and of reaffirming who you really are.
(1134/27)

Through meditation ,*the recognition of one's higher consciousness* (205/25) becomes more familiar. When one becomes better acquainted with one's faculties, they begin to serve one in relation to what one is doing with one's life, because they link one with one's own higher harmony.
(1157/23)

Really there is no such thing as *a higher consciousness* (96/6), *a lower consciousness* (78/6), *an unconscious* (51/6), or *a subconscious mind* (66/3), for *everyone is one consciousness only* (146/11/56). To some these terms are important, to others they are simply convenient ways, more often than not, to avoid looking at something they perhaps fear. (1005/15/6)

Since the Higher Self is our personalized reflection of *the Divine spark* (71/8), *when one feels love from the heart, one is feeling love from one's centralized God space* (356/32/86). This is the point at which one becomes powerful in relationship to others and to one's own being, even to the extent of being able to effect surprising, sometimes magical, health benefits.

(1430/53)

The Higher Self, the soul, does not inhabit - it permeates. It is thought, energy, feeling. It is spirit, and its natural element is ethereal, of the ethers (594/54).

We each have two memories - *the form's (or being's) memory* (122/14/32) and *the soul's memory (or experience)* (140/50). When the latter is allowed to surface one learns that *self-realization* (73/1) is actually *God-realization* (75/3). Knowing more of the Higher Self really means knowing more of God. That inner knowledge is radiant with life, light and love. (1264/32)

Each of us has personalized our perceptions of what we consider reality to be. Each of us has personalized our perception of God and whatever lies within us. Our individual conception of *the Kingdom within* (90/9) can be overwhelming, abstract and non-communicative until we personalize it.

(1150/25)

When we go within and come into alignment with our spiritual power, we come into connection with that spark of Divinity, the Higher Self, the God-within. Whatever one may call it, it is the personalization of *the God source* (59/5) within each of us. (1001/11)

Each being alive is having an *in-the-body experience* (109/19) of his or her own for whatever personal reasons, and each person is as important as each other, and each of us is more important than we seem to ourselves. We are each an aspect of *the great universal intelligence* (140/50), each playing a profoundly important role in *the puzzle that is life* (95/5). (1319/41)

Many people today seem plagued in their personal lives because they are not connected to *the energy of the individual Divine superconsciousness* (243/27/63) (the energy of the

67

Higher Self). My sister, who was dead by the age of fifty, was clearly one of these. Not being able to find the link-up is always tragic; my sister seemed to have a lot going for her earlier on in her life. *The superconsciousness* (89/8), which is connected to *the universal consciousness* (104/5), is speeding ahead, expanding and growing, even as the universe is expanding and growing. I am so grateful to the universe for showing me the link-in. (2398/58)

[Author's note: it is perhaps of interest to realize that my sister, Marjorie Clay, had an expression number 58 (see pg 26).]

The whole point of life is to acquire knowledge of God, and once gained, the life becomes full of nectar. This knowledge is absolutely necessary to man, and one way it can be gained is through Reiki (757/37/73).

Spiritual experiences (104/14) happen only for the growth and benefit of the seeker, and they vary according to the needs of each individual. (556/16/52)

Can spiritual experience be confined within a particular form? Nature always takes its own course: the wind blows, fire burns, water flows - all in their own majestic ways. Just as *God has assumed countless forms in the outer universe* (196/16) *the inner experiences* (107/17) that He gives us are equally diverse. (1096/16)

God takes on a human body and conceals himself within it (204/24). Since it is God who dwells in the body, it follows that a student of Reiki can easily unfold his inner Kundalini.

(633/66/93)

The Power of the Mind (96/6)

The mind is very valuable, so do not underestimate it or think it ordinary. *The mind is the light of consciousness* (152/17/62) in a contracted form. *The mind is the perceptive form of the Kundalini* (211/22/31) and the whole universe has come into being by means of the mind. Likewise the individual lives his life through the agency of the mind.

(1280/38)

A sword is completely actionless in its scabbard; only in battle is it used for cutting or piercing. In the same way *the Kundalini becomes the mind* (119/29) so that the individual soul may experience the fruit of its karma. (802/82)

The mind is the activator of the Kundalini. Take care of the mind for it is a friend that can bring you happiness. But if the mind is corrupted, it will always cause trouble. It will spoil whatever you do and ruin your path to liberation (906/96).

Until your Kundalini is awakened by Reiki, your inner light does not shine, the inner eye of divine knowledge does not open, and your state of bondage cannot be lifted (668/38/65).

The manifestation of the Kundalini (139/49) occurs in an intelligent and totally appropriate way for each person.

(422/44/62)

You Should Meditate (73/1)

God, who lives in your mind, will be quickly pleased and show you his cosmic form in meditation. By the grace of the mind you will easily attain contemplation of the Self (669/39).

Everyone is filled with God in the form of consciousness (244/28/64). Even while you are in meditation He will make your everyday life prosperous and happy. (618/69/78)

Whatever consciousness is, it is pervasive, something found in nature at large with which it shares a basic overall process. It seems tied to the fact of experience (628/61/88).

Meditation is a mind free from thoughts. To free the mind from reflection, from memory and knowledge, to make the mind "not mind", is the nature of *high meditation* (79/7).

(734/14/77)

Examine thoroughly your motives for meditating. Toward what goal are your actions directed? *How much inner faith do you have* (140/50)? What does your mind cling to or seek refuge in? This will indicate your real motives for visiting the *sacred shrine* (66/3). Whatever desire there may be behind your pilgrimage, that will be fulfilled. (1335/48)

The culmination of your search for the objects of the five senses lies in meditation. The culmination of your pursuit for art, poetry, dance, photography, and liberation also lies in meditation. Meditate on *the inner Kundalini* (89/8), by whose power you consider yourself to be you. Seek your own Self.

(1268/35)

As you continue to meditate, the kundalini will open her hidden storehouse and then you will immediately get *higher meditation* (93/3). When this happens *your true beauty will be revealed* (129/39). You will come to know those divine lights that exist inside you. It is this light that husband and wife will see shining in each other. (1262/38)

When beauty is revealed to you, you will see the whole world full of brilliance - its companion sound will also arise. As sound emanates, you hear sweet and divine music. It will chase away your indifference, *your apathy* (53/8), and *the disease of erratic thinking* (138/12/48), as well as the worries of your mind (118/19/28). (1101/21)

The man who loses his sense of himself through meditation, and lets himself merge with his deity, becomes that deity, just as an earring when it is melted down becomes a piece of gold. The man who merges with his deity attains Godhood (208/28).

(809/89)

Truth is rewarded with truth, and falsehood with falsehood, and you must decide what you want. If you want Truth, meditate with truth. Perfect peace is not far away; it lies within your own Self. But first you must be completely pure.

(887/77/86)

You will get the fruit of your meditation in different ways and in varying degrees according to the depth of your feelings, your basic nature, your faith in the Kundalini and your knowledge of its ways, the manner in which you meditate, and the motives behind your meditation (1136/29).

Meditate on that which stills your mind, which frees it from restlessness, and brings it into the Self. Meditate on anything. Through meditation you should attain *the place of supreme peace that is within you* (178/16/88).   (813/84/93)

As meditation deepens the happiness within begins to grow; also one's courage, strength and radiance (390/30).

Through meditation, the mind spontaneously becomes quiet and stable, and the movement of breath becomes more relaxed. When you find *peace within* (59/5), *a new excitement* (62/8) breaks forth in your life.   (737/17/71)

The mind becomes active when it exists separately from the Self (243/27/63). It is this activity of the mind, separate from the Self, that creates *worldly involvement and bondage* (131/14/41). When you see your own mind vibrating in the moving and unmoving universe, the mind ceases its activity and becomes Kundalini.   (1123/25)

In meditation the power of the memory increases. When the mind becomes steady, the prana becomes very pure. Physical torpor is then destroyed and enthusiasm and energy are increased. *The nadis* (35/8) are purified and many sicknesses destroyed.   (950/50)

Meditation is not only for spiritual life; it is also a great friend of the world. As the mind becomes steady, the breath is retained for short periods, which strengthens the nerves, improves blood circulation and digestion, and increases one's alertness. *With regular meditation common ailments can be overcome* (224/26/44).   (1322/44)

71

Arguing is a disease (78/6). Man has suffered from as many diseases in his life and repented. He should then keep away from the disease of controversy about meditation.   (611/62/71)

Meditation is the infallible means of conquering the restlessness of the mind (309/39). It is the wish fulfilling tree which grants whatever you desire, *the magnet which draws the power of God* (168/15/6).   (756/36/72)

One's Perception of the Universe (143/17/53)

The entire universe is the field of the perceived, while the perceiver is *the universal Self* (70/7). The perceived universe exists in accordance with the nature of the perceiver, and is meant only for the perceiver to enjoy.   (918/99)

The universe is the play of the Creator (161/17/71). It is *the play of the universal consciousness* (149/59).   (331/34/61)

He who knows the glory of manifestation as his own, who realizes the entire cosmos in his Self, is divine, even though thought may play in his mind (602/62).

In reality the universe is a divine sport, the playful pastime of Consciousness (315/36/45).

You are the soul of the universe (127/19/37). The changes, permutations and combinations of the universe arise from you; they are yours. As the soul of the universe, you are perfect. Keep on remembering that *the universe is your own grandeur* (150/60).

The inner Self (63/9) is the very essence of that knowledge which bestows the highest bliss, and which has been handed down through the ages.   (522/54/72)

The World in which we live is a play of the self-luminous universal Consciousness (314/35/44). For a man who sees this, *the world is nothing but a play of God's energy* (190/10). For him there is no bondage and no liberation.   (781/61/79)

When you have complete devotion and faith, a firm and

devout Will, and the readiness to surrender everything, then *the energy of the cosmos* (103/13) that comes through Reiki will soon manifest. It takes only a short time for your Reiki Master to open your channel.   (1022/14)

Reiki students must be regular and disciplined. It is necessary for them to live under their control. Otherwise they will not get the full benefit of the energy, and they will fall short of perfection and their growth will be obstructed. (965/92)

There is one thing you must remember: the energy that is active and growing within you is from God (421/43/61).

You should keep Reiki teachings in your heart and follow the path you have been shown. This will be the boat that will carry you across the ocean of worldly existence (648/18/63).

The man who is asleep to the world, but awake to contemplation of the self (100/19), will enjoy *supreme bliss* (50/5) forever. The Reiki student who is filled with eternal bliss is fully worthy.   (666/36/63)

The dedicated and disciplined Reiki student will lead his day-to-day life in the world normally, and even though he may sometimes appear agitated, inside he is supremely peaceful (687/57/66).

When a Reiki student achieves *an understanding of the body* (114/15/24), and sees that it is *the Temple of the Inner Self* (116/17/26), he will never do anything unfriendly to it, nor involve it in anything degrading, nor defile it through depraved or immoral acts.   (976/76)

If you consider everything as *the play of the Divine Consciousness* (145/19/55), you are established in wisdom. Ever free, you have found *the divine joy of the Absolute* (115/16/25). Such a Reiki student is liberated whist still in the body.   (839/29)

When God opened his eyes, the universe was born (193/13),

and when He closes them, it will be destroyed. When God lives within you as your best friend, when He is working within you, when even the briefest meeting with Him makes everything full of warmth and happiness, you must understand how detrimental it will be to forsake His friendship and His delight. (1391/41)

The purpose for intelligent life on earth is for man and woman to reach cosmic consciousness (369/99).

Most people's intelligence is weighted down and slowed by personal considerations and personal love (396/36).

If instead of meditating and studying, you allow your mind to become agitated by quarrels, then the kundalini will gradually become weakened (540/90).

Cosmic consciousness (75/3) is different for woman and man - although finally each complements the other as *one profound perception (120/30/3).* (505/55)

Cosmic consciousness is to participate without interruption in *the intelligence of the universe (144/18/54), the universal scheme for life on earth (161/17/71).* (564/24/51)

There is no difference between you and the world. There is no duality. You fill the whole universe without differentiation. You are the serene, imperishable and pure Kundalini, *the light of consciousness (105/15/6).* (842/32/86)

The universe is the expansion of one's own Kundalini (212/23/32). The illusion you call the universe has arisen in you solely through your own thinking. (537/51/87)

You can perform any number of noble deeds, enjoy any number of pleasures, but as long as your Kundalini is not released, you will never achieve release from bondage (617/68/77).

The Kundalini - the Serpent of Spiritual Fire (190/10)

You should store up the wealth of the Kundalini instead of external riches. *The Kundalini is all-knowing and wise* (142/16/52). The Kundalini knows you are full of feeling and will assist in your finding expression thereof.   (846/36/81)

One bereft of the Kundalini is a transmigratory soul (211/22/31).

Once awakened, the Kundalini does not depend on any support. It is self-effulgent. It freely enjoys its own bliss within itself. It is *the power of the Will* (94/4), resolute and unique, and can perform any miracles it desires. It is *the power of knowledge* (101/11) acting within both the knower and the known. It is *the power of action* (85/4) that produces the energy which creates the innumerable objects of the world.   (1544/68).

Author's note: above add 4 + 11 + 4 = 19. In vibration number 19 one finds the divination *the play of the Divine Consciousness* (145/19/55). This is what the three divinations amount to.

Do You Know God (61/7)?

Have you ever felt *a deep longing in your soul to see God* (152/17/62)? Do you tend to picture God as a long way off - so far away that there appears to be no possible way of bringing Him close to you, or of being led through endless space into His presence? Have you ever felt that it is probably useless even to try to know God as a being - a thinking, loving, conscious and available being?   (1399/49)

Do you go from day to day trying to hold fast to those things that you know are worthwhile, but wishing at times with all your heart that you could feel God nearer to you; that He could come into your home, could speak to you and assure you that He knows and cares (981/99)?

Let us *thank God for His unseen presence* (138/48)! Let us *thank God that He is true to His promise and, though unseen, does not forsake us* (288/18/27), but is nearest when we need Him most, when the struggle to be true to our faith is the bitterest. (808/88)

The human heart (61/7) sees all the lofty qualities which combine to produce the highest and best we can know of manhood and womanhood. These ideally human qualities, we now realize, exist and are possible only because they first exist and continually come forth from God. (1012/13)

True Knowing (58/4)

Some people think they know, but their thinking gets in the way of their knowing. Some people hold on tightly to what they know and get stuck in *the errors of yesterday* (132/15/42). *Some people try hard to prove they know and successfully show how much they don't know* (335/38/65). (1109/11)

Some people work constantly to know, but forget to breathe into their knowing. *The greatest knowing of all is perhaps when you let go of all you think you know* (272/29/92). The most exciting knowing of all is the moment of revelation of *a new level of knowing* (87/6). (963/63)

It is always good to remember that those who know much, know just how much they don't know (196/16). Those who really know are rarely recognized, because they have nothing to prove. Do you know which knower you are? (804/84)

Do You Give or Are You a Taker? (117/18/27)

How many of our relationships are based on giving and how much on taking? How many of us will own up to the fact that we are only abundant givers whilst the other person keeps giving. They have something we want, but we cut off the flow of giving at the very moment we believe there is no more to get (1167/24).

When both terminate *the giving flow* (76/4), each becomes isolated. Time and again both demand more to be given to them by the other. After all, it is their right - that's what you should be able to expect from a husband, wife, parent, child, boss, employee, sexual partner, neighbour or whomever.

(1083/12)

Give me more and I might give you something, but give me more and more and more. Remember that what you receive from me is entirely dependent on what you give to me - that's the universal law, you know! I'm living, but I must make sure you learn it (928/91).

The Drive for More (91/1)

The whole drive for more is spawned by the belief in lack. *The belief in lack is an insidious cancer that eats away at everything and demands constant feeding* (359/89). Its demands are horrendous, and the cost in money terms and on others and on the resources of the planet is mind-boggling.

(1058/14)

A yearning for more is always orchestrated by a devotee of a guru called "lack". We tend to become lackeys of this guru. Being at peace with less comes from being in touch with the rich and prosperous guru that is within each of us. (858/48/84)

The guru that is within (98/8) sees and revels in *the richness of the spirit* (120/30), the miracle of regeneration, the power of love, and the freedom in truth. This is the guru that speaks with clarity, and recognizes that *prosperity means hope* (106/16), and that *a sense of personal wealth means wellness* (135/18/45). *A sense of inner abundance is like a magnet to supply* (184/13/94), and *a sense of inner richness and treasure unlocks the door to giving and loving without conditions* (390/30), and a sense of our own truth allows for discernment in our relationships. (1941/15)

Your Body (46/1)

Some people regard the body as a place of pleasure (66/3), like a club, a hotel or a cinema, and thus destroy its purity and lose their kundalini. (510/60)

The body is the servant of the Self (130/40). It is always at your service and ready to go wherever you take it. If you want to take it to hell, it will go as soon as you ask it. If you want to take it to heaven, it will willingly go there. It is happy with everything. *The body is such a servant, such a slave, such a friend, that there is no one else in the world like it* (357/33/87). (1335/48)

Think of the five primal elements that make up your body. Think of earth which is the womb of many different kinds of food, and the mother of so many different beings. Think of pure water which brings life to grains, fruit, trees and plants; which is so full of love that it washes everything of its dirt and is *the friend of everyone* (113/14/23). Think of fire which lives in all beings according to their needs and is equally the friend of all. In man it becomes the gastric fire and digests food. (1952/17)

Do not be angry with the various limbs of your body (210/30). If you must be angry, then be angry with anger, not with the various limbs of your body. If you listen to what the ignorant may say, do not then harass the limbs of the body for it is *your companion and friend* (119/29). *You get the fruit of all actions in the body* (170/80). *All great persons have become great in the body* (182/11/92). (1369/46)

Let there be only one desire in the body, *the desire for love* (87/6); one wish, to attain *a vision of inner light* (109/19) that will come to you through Reiki; one hope, for *a body that is moderate and disciplined and radiates inner love* (243/27/63).

(889/79)

It is the mind with its *ceaseless thoughts and fancies* (97/7) that takes the body all over the place. *The body runs after thoughts* (114/15/24) and *thoughts run after the mind* (114/15/24). *The mind gives orders to the body and senses* (169/79). So, *why do you punish the body in order to please the mind (231/24/51)?* (960/60)

Your Mind (47/2)

Everyone says that the mind never stays in one place - so true! But have you ever shown it a good place to rest? The Reiki student is shown how to achieve this. *Take the mind to a worthy place and it will stay there* (195/15). It won't wander here and there. (903/93)

If your mind could go deep within yourself, even once, it would stay there (303/33). It has great power, but you will only be able to utilize it if you understand it first. *If you really come to know your mind, you will see what a wonderful worker it is* (319/49). *The mind is a magnificent and creative power* (184/13/94). (1133/26)

The mind wants real love, complete equanimity, and union with God (256/22/76). *The mind wants something captivating; that is why it is restless* (241/25/61). It leaves one place of restlessness and goes on to the next, just like a bee. But there is significant quest behind this restlessness; the mind is looking for perfect repose. (1124/26)

The mind cannot find perfect respose anywhere except in God (259/79). *When you meet God you find everything, and the mind becomes steady* (270/90). Then, even if you try, it doesn't move. It is actually *the restlessness of the mind* (103/13), that has never been satisfied by *temporary stillness* (82/1), which has set you on *the search for truth and peace* (118/19/28).

(1216/37)

Instead of trying to control and force your mind, you should lead it lovingly to *the river of the ecstasy of the Self* (142/16/52). If you turn the mind to *the supremely blissful Self* (104/14), it will want to run there as fast as it can; but if you stubbornly try to make it peaceful by force or austerities, it will become more and more agitated and turn against you.

(1294/34)

To conquer the mind completely you must love it. *Love is a mantra of victory,* (105/15). It is the magnet that draws God to you. (425/47/65)

The Importance of "Love" (96/6)

Love is within you and gives you ever new experiences (232/25/52). Think about *the contentment of deep sleep* (113/14/23). Where does this supersenuous satisfaction come from? When you first meet a friend you feel satisfaction. Where does that come from? Where does *happiness at the sight of beauty* (123/15/33) come from, or *the contentment that sometimes arises spontaneously when your mind is filled with joy* (337/31/67)? If you examine all these questions, you will find that *a source of great contentment is hidden within you. It is supremely blissful and its name is love* (367/34/97).

(2038/22)

The stream of love is already there inside. You just have to spread this love, and in this way it will fill you. The more you give, the more it will grow. *He who spreads his love is welcomed with love everywhere* (247/22/67). (867/57/84)

The lover can see God through love, and through love he can attain *the supremely unattainable* (100/10). (353/38/83)

Show only scenes of love to the witness behind your eyes. Let all your acts be full of love. Love is the mighty *nuclear energy* (69/6) that transforms man. So *do not let your heart become dry* (130/40). Worship love. (739/19)

Love, without desires, craving or attachment, is the key that vanquishes infatuation, enmity and delusion. You don't have to study a lot of scriptures, because *all ideas come from God* (87/6). *It is not a question of knowledge, but of love* (165/12/75). (817/88/97)

Love is your very nature (105/15). *Love is God. Love is the universe* (129/39). *God has appeared as the universe* (124/16/34). The universe is no different. It is the manifestation of the divine Kundalini. (668/38/65)

If you want to unfold *the inner source of love* (105/15), you must first love yourself. *Only love will take you to God* (112/13/22). You desire inner peace, but so often hate your body and senses. You long for inner joy, but so often are *hostile to the body* (78/6), which is a means to that joy, as if it were your worst enemy. You must fully know your body. Once you know your inner being, you will realize that *the body is not illusory, but a beautiful temple filled with knowledge* (266/23/86). By loving it, you will make your own spring of love flow. (1938/12)

If you want to find love, you must have *a true understanding of the body* (128/11/38), the dwelling place of love. (371/11/38)

Love should not be for the satisfaction of the senses or for selfish ends, for then it is just attachment and not love of God. Attachment is impure and can never bring you to God. *Love increases through giving, not through taking* (223/25/43). The feeling of mine and yours is a great obstacle in love. Your love should be equal and unparalleled. (1231/34)

Love is great inner experience (145/19/55). Seek it within. You will feel the divine Kundalini darting with the speed of electricity through your whole body. As you experience it, you

81

will know what love is. (825/15/87)

Man should love his Self, which is all-embracing. He should have complete faith in it. Love turns man into *an ocean of happiness (82/1), an image of peace (65/2), a temple of wisdom (68/5). Love is a man's very self, his true beauty, and the glory of his human existence (292/22).* (899/89)

We are all little cells receiving and transmitting *the Life of Love* (68/5), if we are willing to open our valves. There is nothing vague about this circulation of divine love within and around us. (736/16/79)

The Universal Mind - Let This Be Your Thinking (186/15/96)

The Universal Mind (God) knows all the answers to all problems, and even now those answers that I want are speeding their way to me. I needn't struggle for them, or worry or strive, for when the time comes *the answers will be there (98/8).* (863/53/89)

I know that *I am pure spirit (75/3),* that I always have been, and that I always will be. There is inside of me *a place of confidence and quietness and security (183/12/93).* There all things are known and understood. This is *the Universal Mind, the God (109/19)* of which I am a part, and which responds to me as I ask of it. (1049/14)

Give all problems to *the great mind of God (90/9),* confident that *the correct answers (79/7)* will return when they are needed. Through *the great Law of Attraction (100/10), everything in life that is needed for one's work and fulfilment will come to one (332/35/62).* (920/20)

The hand of the Divine Intelligence (157/13/67) is all around, in the flowers, the trees, the creeks, the paddocks. The same intelligence that created all things is also in everyone, and all persons can call upon it for their slightest needs. (861/51/87)

The body is a manifestation of pure spirit (61/7). As that spirit is perfect, *I dedicate my body to be perfect* (128/11/38). *I intend to enjoy life* (94/4), for each day demonstrates the power and wonder of the universe and myself.   (789/69)

No matter what obstacle or *undesirable circumstance* (95/5) that may cross my path, I will refuse to accept it, for it is nothing but illusion, though it may be a *valuable learning lesson* (88/7). There can be no obstacle or undesirable circumstance to *the mind of God (66/3),* which being in me and around me, serves me all the time.   (1110/21)

Transcendent Experiences (107/17)

The content, significance and particularity of *mystical experiences* (92/2) is that sense of oneness or unity. (456/42/96)

Although so similar to *states of feeling* (64/1), *mystical states* (44/8) seem for those who experience them to be also *states of knowledge* (66/3). They are *states of insight into depths of truth unplumbed by the discursive intellect* (297/27). They are *illuminations* (60/6), *revelations* (50/5), full of significance and importance (1063/19). Persons feeling *part of something bigger* (117/18/27) have variously described their feelings as being at one with the birds, the sea, the grass, the sky; being at one with all creatures; and even being the waterfalls, being the fish, the music, the trees, the road; being a leaf on a tree; being *confronted with the source of all being* (162/18/72).

(1203/33)

The feeling most often experienced is love. It is not just sentimental love as used in everyday language; it is *an overwhelming love* (94/4), *an intense and powerful love* (110/20), *a total love* (33/6).   (665/35/62)

Seeing is the most important sense for a person. Hearing comes next, with touch, smell and taste following in descending order of importance. This seems to be reflected in the fact that there are *so many experiences where something is seen* (191/11), fewer where *something is heard* (84/3), a number where *something is perceived through touch* (173/11/83), very few where smell is involved, and none at all where taste is described. (1453/58)

You crave pleasure, peace and bliss through touch (184/13/94). You seek it in your life, but find only *feverish heat* (63/9). You touch her for *perfect bliss* (53/8), but get only *perfect agitation* (79/7). However, when your inner kundalini unfolds, her love will flow through all your body, and you will experience bliss in every pore. (1224/36)

Some people seeing a light speak of it as a power, a pulsing dynamo, or *a field of energy* (80/8). Sometimes seeing a light seems to be a prelude to the experience of the presence of a figure, or a firm hand on the shoulder. Here, there is an acknowledgment that one is confronted, healed, or otherwise *restored to health* (76/4). (1226/38)

All visionary experiences are external (171/18/81); something outside the person is seen, heard, or perceived. But the trigger appears to be something internal inside the person. The internal factor doesn't need to start the experience, as the person concerned is clearly aware of a state or condition before the experience happens. This very often seems to be *a state of trouble, anguish or stress* (122/14/32). (1542/66)

Many people who experience *a transcendent episode* (85/4) mention the change in their relationship with other people. They become *more tolerant of others* (100/10), have *more empathy* (60/6), are *more humble* (49/4), *more sensitive to the needs of others* (151/16/61). (934/34/97)

The purpose of *a religious or spiritual experience* (171/18/81) is to reveal something that *ordinary consciousness* (101/11) is not able to reveal, or at least not easily for whatever reason. The experience seems to want to reach out to, or give something bigger, greater, more complete than what there is at present. Generally, this is for the sake of others, or for *the common good* (66/3).   (1431/54)

A *transcendent experience* (107/17) has the possibility to alter a person's values. *Values can become hardened or outdated* (134/17/44), and a change may come about only with a jolt.   (548/53/98)

One criterion for assessing the authenticity of a transcendent experience seems to be if it enhances the life and leaves the person better or more whole. Then the person is more likely to use the experience *in the service of others* (108/18).   (926/98)

A *transcendent experience is not magic. People who have had experiences still struggle; they still have pain and suffering. An experience is enhancing* (616/67/76).

Transcendent episodes focus on the need for change (199/19). Perhaps *the unknown or unconscious need for change* (175/13/85) is to become like a child again, so as to be able to take part in life fully.   (658/28/64)

In and through a transcendent experience a person becomes more and more aware, and, given the right conditions, more responsible, active and capable of fulfilling *the creative potential* (93/3). This makes a person more free. He or she is able to know, choose, and act *the values that are relevant* (94/4).   (1100/20)

The Mystery of Life (89/8)

In our heart of hearts each one of us knows that *life is a mystery* (73/1). Where did we come from, where are we going, what is our purpose; and more profoundly still, *what sort of creatures are we, spiritually and physically intermingled as we are* (322/34/52)? We know a great deal about the physical world of which we are a part, and which itself is miraculous and wonderfully constructed, but the glimpses of the other non-physical, spiritual world reminds us that *there is another reality* (113/14/23). (1852/97)

Human beings do not create the meaning in their lives, but they discover it (299/29). This seems to be one of the most urgent tasks of our day. A transcendent experience may be a vehicle for this discovery, but such an experience cannot be wished or conjured into being. It happens when the conditions are right. (1173/21)

The mystery of the transcendent (128/11/38) - why some people have experiences and others do not - is precisely in its illogical appearance and transience, and in the fact that it can only be received, not worked for. (810/90)

There always seems to be a longing and a knowledge that such experiences could have endless uses. Possibly it is not only the experiences that count, but *the developing openness to all things in and around one* (220/40), in particular to *that power beyond oneself* (105/15) that is in one's soul all the time and helps one to indeed see *the invisible* (62/8). (1233/36)

The Question of Belief (96/6)

All of us are beginning to suspect that there is more to us than just the physical form, and that *consciousness can truly expand beyond one's present beliefs* (223/25/43). One may be in *the physical world* (83/2) for a while, and may be able to affect *one's physical surroundings* (120/30) to some degree only. This is what one is taught. (1112/23)

But now one is beginning to discover that one can have a real effect on the overall realities and that *one's thoughts themselves are the actual driving and creative force behind the physical reality* (386/26/35), behind the physical experiences each and everyone has. (998/98)

You have been created with free will (149/59). If you chose to buy into *negative beliefs* (69/63); if you chose to buy into the idea that you can only do just so much and it is beyond your capability to do more, the universe supports you exactly that far and no further, *as the universe never gives more than you say you are ready to handle* (268/25/88). (1235/38)

How many people truly believe that they are ready to handle *absolute infinite unending ecstasy* (138/12/48)? The trouble is that *most people's belief systems are self-regulating* (181/19/91), and that when they do finally create something that seems to be *going the right way* (97/7) they tend to ask themselves how long can this last? (1107/27)

Everything you believe in, you deserve to get (197/17). Deserability is a big issue with most individuals - *I deserve negativity* (95/5), or *I don't deserve positivity* (117/18/27).

(624/66/84)

The Limitation of Guilt (101/11)

The idea of one's willingness to experience *the limitation of guilt* (101/11) actually makes one strong, and is, in and of itself, *an indication of how strong one knows one is* (181/19/91), to be able to subject oneself to limitation.

(771/51/78)

The limitation of guilt allows one to create many wondrous occasions of *self-incrimination* (91/1), *self-validation* (73/1), *self-limitation* (65/2), *segregation* (57/3), and *separation* (46/1) in one's life. It is the primary ingredient, the primary symbol, to allow one to prevent oneself from creating in one's life what one prefers, what one desires, and what one knows deep within one that one deserves to experience in one's life.

(1573/61)

Guilt is what will always perpetuate limitation, always perpetuate separation. It keeps you from recognizing your own *self-empowerment* (72/9) and *your own connection to the*

Infinite Creation (203/23). Guilt is a belief in *the lack of self-worth* (81/9). It stifles creativity and is the denial of your very existence. (1183/22)

Guilt is the bitter pill that was injected into society by society. It keeps you in the status quo of lack of self-empowerment (465/15/42).

Should you truly believe that you are not connected to All That Is (30/3), or *God, the Infinite Creation* (123/15/33); and, when you truly believe you must control by force in order to get anything at all in life; then, do you further *the connection of limitation* (126/18/36), further *the continuation of guilt* (107/17).

Be At Peace and Be Happy (80/8)

If man does not see *the play of the Divine Consciousness* (145/19/55), then no matter what he does he cannot find supreme peace. (423/45/63)

Experiencing that which transcends the individual and makes him a fuller individual, clearly makes the personality more integrated in terms of his place in the world. He will know that there is something outside of him, of which he has been made aware, that broadens his view of life; something that gives him *a widened awareness* (71/8), and brings *thoughts of deity* (78/6). (1433/56)

Remember that cause and effect are the same event. One doesn't have to wait for a reason to be happy in order to know that one prefers to be happy. Create the effect of being happy, and thereby attract into your life all the causes to support the happiness you will have created. (1037/11)

You are not an individual being, you are *The Self* (30/3). All is *your creative energy* (103/13) - outside, inside, above, below. There is nothing other than you. *That which appears inert* (107/17) and *that which appears conscious* (114/15/24) is not

separate from you. This *wisdom and insight* (80/8) brings the greatest peace. It is *the ocean of boundless joy* (91/1).
(1194/24)

Talking of Fate (55/1)

There is no such thing as fate or an accident (166/13/76), for nothing happens in this way. When there appears to be such, what you are recognizing are *overlapping incidents* (106/16), *coincidence* (52/7), that describe the patterns and paths you have chosen for yourself. *Coincidence is a measure of your conscious perception of the simultaneous manifestation of the multidimensional existence of all* (514/55/64).   (1479/57)

Wherever you may find yourself to be, absolutely everything else is there for a reason (362/38/92). So, begin to be fascinated by how well orchestrated everything is that you are participating in - the way you look at someone or he looks at you and even what clothes he or she may be wearing - for *everything is one similar event, albeit experienced from different points of view simultaneously* (427/49/67).   (1531/64)

The idea of coincidence (103/13) becomes meaningful when you allow yourself to recognize that *life always works when you let it* (124/16/34). So, everything you attract in your life is the product of what you believe your life to be. *You can only attract the vibration you are equal to* (189/99), and, whether it is manifested positively or negatively in your life, it is only a reflection of what you believe your reality to be.   (1603/93)

You are always the actual interaction, the actual process. *You are the experience you are having* (170/80). It is not that you are not interacting with other consciousness, but anyone you imagine yourself to be interacting with is generally the only thing you perceive in physical reality. It is *your own self-created version of the individual with whom you are interacting* (337/31/67).

You will always create any interaction in a particular manner (241/25/61), a necessary manner. That manner will always contain any specifics needed by you to see in another individual the things you need to see reflected back to you about yourself. So, in any interaction, you are dealing with *different aspects of your own consciousness* (173/11/83).

(1252/37)

The Shaping of Events to Come (113/14/23)

When you find you are *floating in the limbo state* (103/13), *you are actually at the point of power* (147/12/57) to allow any factor, any event in your reality, to move in the direction and in the style you prefer. When this point is arrived, *you need to act in the direction of preference* (201/21), act *as the representation of the reality you prefer to have* (242/26/62). Things will then fall into place in your life immediately, happening simultaneously. (1661/77)

Never fear to act with the power you have to shape events (220/40). *The creation of your day-to-day reality should be second nature to you* (267/24/87). The only way to get a sense of movement return, and thus know that you are out of any state of limbo, is to have a relative measurement between your own reality and what you can call another reality.

(1191/21)

You are always the creator of your reality, for *any limbo state is your point of power* (158/14/68). It is the living present in the now. Because *you are made in the image of God* (129/39), you are in a sense that powerful. *You are one of the ways the Creation has of expressing itself within the creation* (339/69). In a sense, *as an aspect of the Infinite, you are given the responsibility to create your immediate reality in any way you desire* (487/37/46). (1632/75)

For the Creator to instil free will within you, then at the same time seek to control your life with His will, does not make sense (502/52). You have free will, and you can create any reality you desire which is *made in the image of God* (98/8). Do act as such and you will have *heaven on Earth* (64/1). (1063/19)

Just because there is *a collective limbo state* (79/7), does not mean that you cannot have everything you desire in *your own personal reality* (116/17/26) now. The more you create the reality you desire to live in now, the faster will you represent a living example to everyone else as to the type of reality they can create collectively also. This will speed the whole process. It is, as always, in your own individual hands. (1531/64)

In the Present (63/9)

Everything is happening now, and there is only *the present* (49/4), *the past* (26/8), and *the future* (43/7), created out of the present. You cannot make a conscious decision that doesn't affect the reality you are deciding about. It is not a question of *predicting the future* (103/4), it is more that *you are sensing the energy at the present* (171/18/81) that appears most likely to occur in the future, as it has *the greatest degree of energy* (134/17/44) behind it. But, it is only because you are aware that a life programme already exists in the now, that you can make such a prediction. (2011/22)

You cannot make a *conscious decision* (80/8) that doesn't affect the reality you are deciding about. *Every thought changes the reality you are thinking of* (241/25/61). *So-called predictions manifest in due course* (392/32). The prediction itself, of course, changes the energy. Should what has been sensed have *a great deal of energy momentum* (123/15/33) behind it, it will be *unlikely to change* (76/4). (1483/52)

Whenever your life appears to be in a limbo state, things will only be seemingly standing still because you will have caught up with the speed of your creation. In other words, you are *in perfect equilibrium* (115/16/25) with the rate at which you are creating your reality.   (1076/14)

Whenever *inertia* (40/4) is balanced, everything has the equal ability to be moved by you in whatever direction you prefer. So, in such *a period of standstill* (84/3), where it may seem you have done all you can do, it is actually *the time when things can begin to happen most magically* (221/23/41), most quickly. The only reason that it may not seem to be doing so is because you are standing there waiting for something to happen.   (1537/61)

External Channelling (87/6)

Most channelling involves connections with *disembodied forms of consciousness* (140/50). Channelling is really only the process of allowing more of one's typical day-to-day personality to come through in *a free-flowing stream of consciousness* (150/60) in a very creative way.   (1027/19)

Because the information that comes through channelling seems to be valid for many people, they can make changes in their lives the way they want. Each must decide for themselves if the data is something they want to use.

(816/87/96)

The channelling process (98/8) helps one to wake up and regain the power to take back responsibility for the creation of one's life (488/38/47). *Energetic daydreaming* (106/16): feeling the energy that is coming through (301/31).

The Energy Frequency (108/18)

A society that is full of people that hide things for themselves has created *gaps in the energy field* (112/13/22), and is *vibrating at a very low and slow frequency* (171/18/81).

(591/51)

The people who are willing to be their full selves operate *at a higher frequency* o(100/10). The analogy of a fast spinning gear and a slower turning gear is interesting. Bring the two together without matching frequencies and *there will be a disruption* (112/13/22). (1051/16)

By the definition of integration, one can get to *highly accelerated places* (105/15) very quickly. (374/14/32)

The Spiritual Path (77/5)

You are at the beginning of a spiritual path, which is characterised by *difficulty or chaos* (88/7). You must realize that just as *chaos lies at the heart of order* (125/17/35), so *order lies at the heart of chaos* (125/17/35). (718/79/88)

A person developing spiritually is aware of *a creator behind the gigantic scenes of the universe* (215/26/35). Some are enthralled with the forces and energies of cosmic life. Often, however, *a revelation is needed* (88/7) to make clear the wonders of time and eternity. (974/92)

You must organize *your spiritual search* (96/6) as if you were an army preparing for war. You must have *a clear objective* (59/5), then mobilise all your forces to achieve it. Let all your activity stem from a single cause - *your aim for enlightenment* (125/17/35). (918/99)

The turnaround in your life may, alas, sometimes take quite a dramatic event to cause one to change one's thinking and priorities (477/27/45).

The world is a school (80/8), and all our worldly life is only a preparation for the *real life of eternity* (114/15/24). The only reality is in *the spiritual world* (86/5), of which we become conscious at death. (731/11/74)

Sometimes it takes *a tragedy or shock* (73/1) to awaken a person to *a spiritual need* (64/1) in their life. (336/39/66)

It is "the now" that is important, providing, as it does, *an opportunity to change the detrimental aspects in one's character* (269/89), so that the future will be enhanced.

Always remember that God is the spirit that breathes life into all living organisms in the world, and leaves them with a degree of freedom to explore the possibilities of reaching their potential (721/73/91).

Life is well worth fighting for, so one shouldn't be passive about it. It is very special and precious, and who knows if one will get another chance at it or not (641/11/65)?

It is heaven all the way along, if one makes it so and raises *the tone of the soul* (73/1) into that *perfect health* (64/1) where nothing can worry or distress it. (554/14/59)

Destiny is not a matter of chance. It is a matter of choice. It is not a thing to be waited for, it is a thing to be achieved (445/49/85).

One cannot change destiny already made. It is the field of action, provided by one's thoughts. The future may be changed by submitting to the destiny already provided, by changing one's thinking, and by working out new duties (504/54). (874/64/82)

Are you willing to make sacrifices in other areas of your life in order to gain *the maximum amount of spiritual growth* (163/19/73)? (496/46)

The Path to Good Health and Healing (159/69)

- Always that healing occurs in another dimension. It is beyond time and space. It doesn't need to take long (424/46/64).

- There must be a commitment to help yourself. You must be prepared to make changes (292/22).

- There must be an investment of time. Learn to be selfish. Then you should have time to relax

(331/34/61).

- Learn to laugh, stimulating endorphin in the brain. There is a direct link between seriousness and stress (408/48).
- Being spiritually reborn will lead to new tissue growth. This is healing (302/32).
- With greater personal comfort, you will have greater energy to share (209/29).
- The resolving of inner turmoil or conflicts is a signpost. It leads to healing (308/38).
- How good are you at giving and receiving compliments, for with a closed heart chakra, the giving and receiving of compliments will be difficult (709/79)?
- When things in your body change, things in your life will change, and vice versa. Therefore don't allow stress to become part of any illness. This only allows cancer a chance to creep up and grab you (866/56/83).
- Always reflect that when feelings and emotions are not allowed, sickness or disease is likely to follow. Any emotional attitude which is attached to a habit can lead to frustration. So, always look inside and see what the source is, because it will be you that has developed the condition (1012/13).
- All too often, one is reluctant to improve a relationship problem or a health problem. It becomes a matter of living with stress (506/56).
- Do you say one thing with your tongue and another thing with your body (275/23/95)?
- Reflect on your emotional conditioning, for the conscious mind is programmed by one's parents and teachers. Sometimes they may be "screwed-up"

themselves. Also, established "belief systems" are responsible for setting minds (808/88).

- Bring relaxation, music, humour, and breathing into your life. Also let feathers into it, for when you find one from a bird, it will have appeared at a turning point in your life (734/14/77).
- You must have somewhere to go, and there must be more than one spot (241/25/610).
- Learn to think and act positively, to give, to release, and to love (235/28/55).
- Learn to be happy, and do not mind if others copy you (282/12/21).

The purpose of life (88/7) is not to abolish or destroy any of the various selves within us, but to get them to work together in harmony (122/14/32), and to put any evil selves under the control of the good. (722/74/92)

When you can understand that your lifestyle was a big part in how your disease got going, how the illness came about, then what your life is saying is that a big part of your difficulty is how you deal with stress (786/66/75).

The world of spirituality (118/19/28) is a world of non-ordinary reality. *Those who are healthy and happy will be those who achieve longevity* (287/17/26). A sensitivity will be involved, to others, rather than to the Self. (812/83/92)

Doubt not in your own ability (120/30), for you have *the power to receive* (95/5), just as you have *the power to give* (80/8), and as you trust in your own process, *the knowledge and wisdom will flow* (126/36), and you will become at one with *the vital force* (63/) that is within you. (908/98)

The development of absolute faith in goodness and the power of the Self, together with the constant and energetic cultivation of optimism, is what you must aim for (644/14/68).

The Easy Road (51/6)

What is it about *skating on the surface* (81/9), about *travelling down the easy road* (119/29), that seems so appealing and can snare us so badly. The appeal to skating on the surface is both *the release from pain* (91/1) and *the promise of pleasure with no strings* (171/18/81) - in other words "sense experience". (1012/13)

The Experience Called "Life" (116/17/26)

Life is, or should be, one continual celebration with many powerful rites of passage marking *the way to deeper and deeper levels of knowing and feeling* (238/22/58), connected to the whole, thereby increasing one's confidence to live more fully. (933/96)

Nothing you see in the mirror is negative. Everything should be viewed as gift that will bring *self-awareness* (48/3), for after all you are here to learn, for if you were already perfect, you wouldn't be here. (822/12/84)

Life in the human body affords opportunity by which the doer is taught, trained, and disciplined to be in union with his triune self (545/59/95).

The triune Self - the indivisible self-knowing and immortal one - its identity and knowledge part as *knower* (32/5); its rightness and reason part as *thinker* (40/4); and its desire and feeling part as doer (24/6). (725/77/95)

The foundation for life (106/16) should be built on the understanding that there is *a higher intelligence, a fundamental creative power or energy* (273/21/93) in the universe, which is the source and substance of all things. (816/87/96)

To reject *the shadow side of life* (94/4), to pass by with averted eyes, refusing our share of *common sorrow* (64/1) while expecting our share of *common joy* (42/6), would cause the unliked, rejected shadows to deepen in us as fear, including our fear of death.   (907/97)

On *the emotion level* (76/4), it is our *resistance to feeling* (89/8) that causes us pain. If, because we are afraid of a certain feeling, we suppress it, we will experience *emotional pain* (63/9). If we allow ourselves to feel it and accept it fully, it becomes *an intense sensation* (73/1), though not a painful one. If a sensation isn't really dangerous, you can relax into it and the pain will diminish and dissolve.   (1424/56)

Every individual has free choice in the selection of a lifestyle. However, he must never complain if events sooner or later turn against him (578/38/56).

When you see *beauty everywhere* (86/5), it is a *reflection of yourself* (106/16). There are mirrors everywhere. Whatever or whoever you have a connection with is a mirror for you, and the deeper the connection, the stronger the mirror.   (960/60)

The main sign that you are following your intuition in your life is *increased aliveness* (76/4). It feels like *more life energy is flowing through your body* (227/29/47). It may even feel a little overwhelming, like *more energy than your body can handle* (161/17/71).   (986/95)

When one intuitively comprehends and factually grasps the concept that spirit and matter are one reality (137/11/47), and once one achieves within himself *the sublimation of matter* (95/5), then one can divorce oneself from all that the human being understands in relation to form.   (1023/15)

Anyone who has succeeded in developing an awareness will get progressively drawn onto and along *the path to the Light* (85/4).   (470/20)

The Light (44/8) - that seemingly illusive force that is always available, even *in the dark* (45/9).   (305/35)

Spiritual wisdom (73/1) will be gained through careful

observation of people and things, and *worldly success* (56/2) by *learning through experience* (146/56/11). The strength comes from overcoming disappointments in early life, and possessing the rare quality of learning from past mistakes.

(1096/16)

Through some philosophical or *metaphysical discipline* (108/9), you can more easily tap into *your great potential* (89/8). (470/20)

Should one abuse one's *developing powers* (88/7), the result will be unpleasant, but infinitely less than *the abuse of the higher powers* (133/16/43), *the karmic reward* (76/4) of which is *spiritual death* (64/1). (689/59)

As long as one has one central thing which is constant in one's life, one should afford to surround oneself with change in all other areas (529/79).

Achieving Your Goal (93/3)

The evocation of a deeper consciousness (153/18/63) requires a thinning out of the various processes to assist, including Reiki. Never lose the sense of depth of who you are, and what you can do to or for others. (807/87)

You must neutralise your feelings towards people who happen to influence your life negatively. You must never allow hatred to enter your mind or heart, for hatred, like love, is a form of *subjective involvement* (87/6) that binds you to the object or person you hate. You must learn how to retreat quickly into the *inner realms of thought* (119/29) where hatred cannot reach. (1412/53)

Reflect that hatred, like anger, both poisons the mind and sours the stomach (281/11/19).

By giving attention to the fact that *aggressive thoughts* (86/5) are meaningless, one learns not to hate, not to create *destructive realities* (91/1) within one. An emotion such as hatred does not help one to act properly. One doesn't need to be indifferent to *hateworthy actions* (82/1). Instead, try saving your energy by acting *intelligently and creatively* (127/19/37).

(1310/41)

Always evoke *the alternative solution* (96/6) and stop harking back to any problem. (270/90)

Retreat is not dishonourable. It is *a strategic withdrawal* (87/6). Fate could be against you at the moment. (362/38/92)

The awakening of the Kundalini purifies the seeker (214/25/34), it rids him of all his old impressions, blocks, and impurities (155/11/65). Because these vary from person to person, the process is unique for everyone. (783/63/72)

The Kundalini is the essence of Aum. When awakened, lives which had seemed commonplace and arid, unenjoyable and frustrated, become *gay and flourishing,* (91/1) filled with sweetness, contentment and delight (736/16/79).

On the Subject of *"Creation"* (40/4)

Within the creation of the universe, there is nothing that insists that a *conflict situation* (76/4) is any more real than one that has no conflict. So, it is your choice out of habit when you believe that pain is more real than joy. *So many people seem to believe that they cannot have anything in their life that is worthwhile, unless they have suffered* (486/36/45).

(1349/44)

You were created out of ecstasy. You were created out of love and light. It is your birthright. *You are made in the image of the Infinite Creator,* (212/23/32); and that means that *you yourself are an infinite creator* (162/18/72). (790/70)

If you allow yourself *the expressiveness of your vitality* (155/11/65), you will then be able, with all clear consciousness, to create and attract into your life the things you know you deserve. *You are not given a desire by the Infinite Creator without also being given the ability to accomplish that desire* (472/22/49). (1154/29)

So grant yourself permission, and grant yourself the right to create life as you desire it to be, for you have the ability to create it that way. All you have to do is to remind yourself that your ability to conceive that idea is, in and of itself, the indication of your ability to create the idea. (1143/27)

You must realize that *your physical reality is always the product of what you believe it can be* (276/24/96), or of what you fear it will be. To fear that something will happen in your life, simply suggests that you believe that *the fearful scenario* (84/3) *is the strongest possible reality* (125/17/35) likely to come into your life. (1167/24)

Situations do not happen in your life to show that you are stuck in them, nor do they happen to show that you have failed to create better ones. *Situations occur to show you what beliefs you have been taught, or what beliefs you may have bought into* (386/26/35). So, it is your prerogative if you don't like them to change them. And, if you like them, you may reinforce them. (1387/46)

Each and every person has *a self-regulating mechanism* (107/17) to know what beliefs may be buried in their unconscious minds. *It is through the regulation of your subconscious mind, which is your very own God, that you may change any belief you want to* (468/18/45). It is always better, of course, to effect change later than never. (1204/35)

Coming to Terms With Society (122/14/32)

All of us are born with a total facility for living life in absolute joy. However, society drums that joy out of most of us by a very early age. As a result, *you begin to buy into the belief systems that society deems are the belief systems one should buy into in order to survive in the world* (525/57/75). (1089/18)

101

Society chose a group consciousness highly focussed into *physical materiality* (95/5). With changing times, people are awake now that *there is something more to life* (141/15/51), and thus, there is now an opportunity to return to *the cycle of joy and creativity* (127/19/37). This is the start of the transformational life. Every single day brings *new connections to different levels of consciousness* (206/26).   (1471/58)

It is important to recognize that you have chosen your purpose in being in this society at this time on the planet. Know that, *if you were not going to make a difference, you should not be here* (264/21/84). Begin to understand that each and every individual makes a difference within society as a whole.   (1139/23)

The Energy Fields (83/2)

Know that you are connected through *the mental fields* (63/9) you create on the planet, through *the physiological fields* (115/16/25) you create, through the manipulation of *the energy field* (82/1) of the planet itself. All mental, physiological, emotional, and spiritual ideas are diversifications out of the same primal, homogenous energy field, *the primal consciousness* (97/7).   (1372/49)

Many different layers have been created by you out of the homogenous oneness of the energy field. Recognize that because you are creating the diversification, you are still connected to every single layer. All layers are within you, so every move you make within yourself is a move made in *the outer physical awareness, because the outer physical reality is only a reflection of every idea you are exploring within the Self* (425/47/65).   (1722/84)

Always be in touch with the fact that the so-called future is always fluid. There are many probable realities. If something is going to happen and is expected to be catastrophic, it is simply a perception of a one band-width frequency, one probable reality. As *there is always energy behind the probable future* (208/28), if you don't prefer it, you don't have to stay on that frequency. (1441/55)

Individuals, who understand that they can use energy to enlighten themselves and accelerate themselves in a positive way, will alway stay abreast of any changes in the global economy, or due to the impending electromagnetic axis shift. *There are always shifts in energy taking place, both in the beings and in the planet, since in a sense they are both the same thing* (493/43). (1380/48)

Transforming the Self (94/4)

A lot of the idea of someone experiencing *a transformation* (67/4) in a negative way is that he or she is *holding on tight to an old belief* (138/12/48), and will not allow himself or herself to let go and trust *life's natural flow* (68/5). It all too often seems to take even a degree of violence to break the grip.
(1069/16)

Any time you are made aware of an idea which appears to be presented in a *potentially negative form* (116/17/26) do not take it as *an absolute prediction* (88/7). Regard the idea as an opportunity to which you can be attracted, and then proceed to vibrate around it with *positive energy* (83/2). *Experience any opportunity, any exploration, any excitement, rather than any negative anxiety or fear, limitation or segregation* (565/25/52). (1633/76)

Whatever way you choose to vibrate will be the reality you get, for never does a circumstance have in-built meaning, for all situations are fundamentally neutral. You give them meaning. *You experience the reality of the way you vibrate, for you cannot experience the reality of the way you do not vibrate* (498/48). (1197/27)

Whenever a prediction is made, the individual making the prediction is sensing the energy as it lies at the moment (471/21/48). You always have the opportunity to change that energy. You must appreciate that the reason any prediction exists is to let you know where the energy is considered to be. Then if you prefer it isn't there, you simply change it.

(1400/50)

Your own awareness of where the energy lies effectively changes the energy for, if you don't prefer it to be there, you can do something about it by focussing your consciousness on it. Should you hear a prediction where you feel unable to change the energy, you generate fear which acts to reinforce that energy,making it more likely that the prediction will come to pass. But always remember that *any prediction in no way determines that this is the absolute thing which must happen* (349/79), so there remains a great deal of flexibility with regard to the prediction. (2280/48)

Never ever regard any prediction as being cast-iron (226/28/46). Regard it is an opportunity to examine where the energy lies. If you don't prefer it to be there, take it as *an opportunity to change* (108/18) it by doing the things that excite you, being of service, or acting as though you deserve ecstasy. (1191/21)

Always endeavour to utilize every situation in a sharing way, and not in an accusatory way (339/69). *Stand up and be seen to make a difference* (134/17/44) be the individual you know yourself to be, and express what you know to be true for you. Everyone will benefit from this. (957/57/93)

Even as a single individual, *you can add that much energy to the momentum of your ability to experience your transformation in a positive and loving way* (506/56). For each of you is energy and experience it you will. You yourself are the experience you are having. (1056/12)

104

That Soul of Yours, That Spirit (114/15/24)

Begin to allow yourself to recognize that in a non-physical state you are not human - you are quite something else. *You are an essence, a primal idea of energy consciousness, a soul that can project itself as basically any form, any symbol, any idea it wishes to* (507/57). Understand that the soul, the energy essence, is not intrinsically human. Thus you can begin to understand yourself in a homogenous sense, as everything and nothing at the same time, as a principle, as an idea, as an essence. (1745/89)

What society refers to as *the second coming* (73/1) is not the coming of an individual. It is the recognition within each individual of *the Christ that each and everyone is* (145/19/55) and, then, living like it. (772/52/79)

God is spoken of as being omnipotent (146/11/56), everywhere and all-knowing, omniscient and all-seeing, everything and everywhere. *If God is everything, how then can you be outside of it* (229/49)? You must also be God, and God must also be you. *God knows you are God* (84/3). Why then do you not know that you are God? (1106/26)

A sinner - someone who is outside of, has placed himself outside of, his recognition of himself as God (400/40).

The Holy Spirit is the collective electromagnetic mentality (255/21/75), the actual energy out of which all individual minds are created. Spirit is a physiological phenomenon, an electrical phenomenon, an electromagnetic phenomenon. *It is the literal light of the world and of consciousness* (201/21).

(1138/22)

Your Desire Will be "Your Energy Level" (170/80)

All of us are as powerful as we need to be to create anything

we desire in life (289/19), without having to hurt anyone else
or oneself in order to create it. *Believe in the power you are as
the reflective representation of the Infinite Creator* (376/16/34).

As you think, as you picture, as you imagine, that is real.
*Be it, if you prefer what you imagine, and that will be the
reality you experience* (340/70).   (1470/57)

All anyone needs is a basic trust that they will have what
they need. They need to know everything they need to know
to be what they are being at any given moment. When they
redefine who they are, they will know the things that person
needs to know, regardless of what they are seeing around
them at the present. *The way to change things in the world
quickly is to change the idea of who one is* (328/31/58).

                                                          (1486/55)

Know that you cannot change anything out there. You can
only allow other people and situations to change. *If you wish
to see anything in the world change, change yourself*
(273/21/93).   (672/42/69)

When listening to the radio one hears the station that one is
tuned into. Therefore, *create the image of what you prefer and
live accordingly at that frequency* (310/40). You will be the
receiving beacon for that energy, so that programme is able to
be broadcast within this worldly reality, and others can pick
up on it and decide to tune their dial to that frequency as
well. If others don't know that such a programme exists, how
can they tune their dials to your frequency?   (1814/95)

If you know you have initiated a certain vibratory energy
(126/18/36), *a certain excitement* (81/9), and you see it
progressing in a certain way, and then all of a sudden it
changes, why give it the meaning that it has stopped? Why
not give it the meaning that it is still going on, but on another
frequency which is perhaps necessary to attract to you the
individuals you originally wanted to attract in the first place,

but were not succeeding in so attracting them by the original way you were doing it. (1915/16)

Look on life as a continuing series of energy interchanges (250/70), making all the connections to the different vibrations you want to connect to. *Interchanging energy* (115/16/25) is necessary to transform into *different frequencies* (110/20), to attract individuals who think differently to the way you do. If you truly trust what you are doing is representative of who you choose to be in this life, then no matter how *the energy changes* (85/4), no matter in what way the excitement continues, the fact that *the excitement* (61/7) does continue is the sign that *your life is on course* (96/6).

(1025/17)

If you allow yourself to know that you are following the path at any given moment that you have created for yourself, you will then be more strongly *in touch with all the different levels of your consciousness* (240/60). That, in itself, will tell you that you do not need as much *unconscious time* (65/2) in which to connect to those levels during sleep, because you are doing it consciously. (1415/56)

Any time you live right in *the now* (31/4), utterly in the moment, any energy that comes along, any difference you feel, you will match instantly, due to *living fully in the now* (106/16), accepting it all, open to it all, through *absolute vulnerability*. Such is not weakness but openness, strength, *self-empowerment* (72/9). (1128/21)

Any blockages that appear are there for a reason (181/19/91), and the sooner you become conscious of them the better, for they are there to allow you to accept the energy and accelerate once more. (710/80)

When you project yourself into *physiological reality* (110/20), and then determine through *non-physical consciousness* (106/16) that you will create certain types of experience, that is *the meaning* (51/6) you are giving to the particular life you are creating for yourself as a *non-physical entity* (90/9), to experience as *a limited physically focussed entity* (151/16/61). (1216/37)

Such is the meaning that is your overall desire, which by vibrating at a certain frequency, calls out of *the background vibration* (104/14) through *a sympathetic synchronisation* (138/12/48), all the circumstances necessary to represent the meaning injected into the general physical life theme or structure which you are about to experience. (1245/39)

To Give Meaning is to Create (112/13/22)

All circumstances are neutral. *The meaning you choose to believe; the meaning you choose to create in your life, about your life, is what generates the particular type of circumstances you experience* (665/35/62). These reinforce, reflect and represent the meanings you are creating. *To give meaning is to effectually undertake an act of creation* (233/26/53). (1290/39)

You are a definer (75/3), ultimately, of the life you experience. As you define it, as you give it meaning, your life takes on, and can only take on, the colouration, the flavours, the characteristics and the atmosphere of the meaning you decide your life is to have. (1014/15)

You do not have to see yourself as a struggle against, or between, this and that, for you have at any given moment, *free will of preference* (116/17/26). For example, if you recognize that the idea of *continual nibbling between meals* (122/14/32), or perhaps of *continuing to smoke* (80/8), does not vibrate with the being you prefer to be, then if you act like *the preferred being* (102/12), you should find that particular urge melts away, as you are not of the vibration containing the urge. (1762/88)

To achieve the giving up of a habit, all that you have to do is to *change the belief that changing is difficult* (187/16/97). The changing of the belief that having the concept of what you would prefer to be, is not the same thing as being it.

(973/73/91)

If you find it difficult to hold a new belief or concept, you must appreciate that this in itself is a belief and its own reality, and therefore what you get - a reality where you are *a being who finds it difficult to hold a concept* (190/10). Remember that *all fixed habits are breakable* (105/15), if you identify the habit and then really believe that *you have the ability to change* (121/13/31).   (1391/49)

You may sometimes feel that you are wandering off your path. This is not possible because *a path is what you are* (76/4), and *you can't wander off yourself* (114/15/24). Everything you do is an opportunity to decide what you prefer - everything. *You can learn from everything* (136/19/46).

(1016/17)

Every situation has the potential for you to learn something from it in whatever way you may wish (403/43). When you are as clear as you can be about the definition of *the life you have bought into* (122/14/32), then every situation can be used to see how it matches up to those preferred definitions. Where it doesn't appear to work for you, you can take advice, and where it does so work for you that's fine.   (1488/57)

The major step in creating the reality of what you desire to be is to *cease invalidating yourself* (114/15/24), for you are the only thing you have to work with in the universe - *a representative in your own way of the Infinite* (215/26/35). *By invalidating say part of you, you are not allowing yourself to function as a whole being capable of utilizing information coming from others in a constructive way* (676/46/64).

(1589/68)

Chapter 4

Spiritual Energy is the Key to Life Enrichment

Being a forester by training, I have always had a tremendous respect for the *inherent energy* (103/4) within trees, which have the capability of even growing to 300 feet in height under a great variation of weather conditions.

Because I had personally developed *ringing in the ears* (96/6) which I was determined to rid myself of, even though it is said to be incurable, I began to investigate both *crystal energy* (68/5) and *magnetic power* (68/5) with gratifying results, because I finally got on top of my health difficulty.

Once one starts investigating nature's own secrets (68/5), one seems to get drawn further and further. This is what happened with me.

I then found myself invited to a national seminar run by Mahikari. The Mahikarians have a hands-off technique for dispensing *Light* (29/2). One goes along to sessions lasting about an hour at the headquarters, where one receives Light starting always on *the neck: the ultimate store of tension and the bridge between the wisdom in the body and the knowledge in the head* (440/80/8).

It wasn't long before my attention was directed to Reiki, a hands-on healing technique. *The gift of healing* (89/8) comes through a series of *energy attunements* (75/3) given by the Reiki Master Teacher. Once one has become what is termed *a Reiki Channel* (65/2), one has the healing ability for the rest of one's life. With Mahikari, one has to return time and again to be "recharged with Light".

Since becoming a Reiki Master Teacher, I have gone on to investigate *Kofutu symbols* (48/3) and the methodology that is known as *chelation* (42/6). Now I incorporate both Reiki and Kofutu with my teachings.

There is no doubt that the Reiki technique can prove to be very effective in *opening up one's channel to The Universe* (165/75/3). *Use of the Kofutu symbols greatly enhances personal growth* (226/28/46). There is no doubt that *improved physical healing occurs when chelation is used* (240/60).

The simple fact of life is that *no one can be fit and well unless they are able to access the earth's energy upwards through their feet* (379/19/1). Thus there is a lot to be said in favour of chelation.

As presently taught, the Reiki technique certainly gives one what might be termed *a spiritual uplift* (75/3). Ascending to "Cloud Nine" is great, but if the rise is too quick there is always the danger of coming down sooner or later with a bump.

Incorporating chelation with Reiki on a person, David, who had his thyroid removed some time ago, the amount of energy that showed up in his throat chakra, where the thyroid is situated, was most impressive. I do not believe that this would have occurred without accessing *the earth's healing energy* (119/29) by starting at the feet and working upwards.

Like everything else in life Reiki must change with the times, for there is an obvious need for any technique that benefits health in the way Reiki does to become more accessible to the public. This is now starting to happen as Independent Reiki Masters lower the cost for learning Reiki.

Shaktipat is a Hindu term associated with *the raising of the Kundalini* (124/16/7). It is normally dispensed by a Guru. However, I was fortunate enough to be recommended to read the book *"Play of Consciousness"* by Swami Muktananda. It is a forceful book. In it the writer says that it is possible for a reader of the book to receive Shaktipat, whilst reading the book.

From my early days, I rejected all the religious teachings thrust before me. So you can perhaps imagine how surprised I was to realise that, in reading the book, I had *a meeting with God* (79/16/7). Yes, indeed, I received Shaktipat. Later, after meeting with Gurumayo, I became a devotee of Siddhah Meditation. And so, *my energy level* (73/1) further increased.

I think it is important to appreciate that *energy just doesn't happen, it has to be worked at. You cannot pick it up at a corner store, nor can you acquire it from someone else. As your level of awareness rises so does your consciousness and along with this your energy level* (857/47/2).

What is this energy, this light? Religious philosophies have expressed the importance of light. One is told *you are the light of the world* (129/39/3). This is an energy statement familiar to many. *Reiki is a life-light energy* (137/47/2).

With respect to Reiki herewith some divinations:

Reiki is life-light energy which in its pure existence is light (299/29/2). *In applying Reiki, you are applying natural light energy from the outside and promoting internal healing and wholing* (527/59/77/2).

The transmission of energy in the Reiki technique puts one in touch with a concentrated beam of light which promotes the restoring, renewing and balancing of natural life-force energy throughout the body (879/69/6).

In its outer form Reiki is the technique for applying and directing *light energy* (69). Perhaps it would be better to know it as *the manifestation of the Great Spirit* (159/69). In its inner form, *Reiki is a contact with the metaphysical light source* (215/26/35). There is a link between light and the mental and physical health of humans.   (1209/39/3)

With the Reiki technique you can apply its basic principles to any *energy imbalance* (73/1) or disease you may be experiencing. It is possible to obtain relief from allergies, arthritis, general debility including headaches and many other more serious imbalances.   (1062/18/9)

Reiki is a profound tool for *growth and transformation* (113/14/23) and a gentle, subtle, yet *powerful healing* (82/1) art and science. Reiki gives you a direct way of contacting and applying *natural energy* (64). The basic tenet of wholistic health and living is the acceptance of responsibility for your own health, sense of *wellbeing* (44) and *evolving consciousness* (92).   (1292/32)

Reiki reduces and releases *negative stress* (57/3) whilst promoting positive stress (62/8), the essential key to *balanced energy* (64/1), *positive wellness* (71/8), wholeness and even *enlightenment* (65/2).   (624/66/84)

Reiki is a contact with *natural energy* (64/1). It is a way of activating and amplifying the power within you. Being natural and *energy balancing.* (76), it is both safe and easy to use.   (649/19)

Through the centuries, *the information of how to contact Light was preserved and concealed in symbols* (308/38). Reiki is the rediscovery of an ancient healing technique. It is an art and science of Light that now acts as *a tool for transformation* (105/6).   (891/81)

The opening up of a person's channel to the universe, and thereby the activating of *a higher level of metaphysical energy* (172/19/82), needs only a living transmitter and a living receiver. The transmission or attunement is done by one person to another. The Reiki Master Teacher has mastered the knowledge preserved in the symbols rediscovered by Dr Usui.   (1361/47)

Useful Energy Indicators

- *The Pranatic Total: the energy contained in the pranatic total is like a sleeping volcano* (341/35/71). (Add together the Expression and Motivation numbers of the full name plus the Destiny number).
- *The Activator (the Sutraman): this golden thread of individuality is a stream of self-consciousness on which are strung the life principles* (548/53/98). (Add together the Expression Number of the Christian name and the day of birth).
- *The Spiritual Seal: exposes the hidden desires of a person* (230/50). (Add together the total number of each vowel in the full current signature).

As individuals gain skill in tapping their inner self, of touching into their source, their inner world becomes definite, sure and safe territory. Until a person thinks and knows from his inner source, he cannot be an intelligent, wise and compassionate participant in the unfolding that is going on everywhere in the universe (1353/48).

As you become increasingly conscious of *the flow of the universe* (103/4) moving through everything and everyone else, your body will become capable of channelling more energy. The more energy you are willing to receive, the more you will be able to give.   (1103/23)

The Great Divine Spirit (112122/13)

Dia ko mio is the symbolic key to accessing the great spirit and thereby activating the power within each of us.
(447/42/87).

Somewhere in our journey through life, each of us has some experience of our true *Inner Self* (48/3). This experience is individual for each of us, relating as it does to the particular circumstance of our upbringing. From such knowledge of the *inner dimension* (96/6) one begins to grow. (1154/29)

In the search for harmony, the accessing of nature's energy will make life easier (332/35/62).

To fully appreciate Light, it is necessary to first experience and understand darkness (341/35/71).

It is only at *the spiritual level* (79/7) that one may readily access energy. (261/27/81)

Spiritual growth is the only purpose and reason for being alive on the planet. Every individual must learn to utilize energy for spiritual growth and constructive purposes. This raises the level of consciousness of man (913/94).

When you focus on *the universe inside* (89/8), you can have everything: money, success, fulfilling relationships, as well as that incredible connection inside. (607/67)

The more sensitive the form-mind becomes to the unseen, the more sensitive one becomes and the more one sees in the visible (517/58/67).

The natural harmonies contribute to the preservation of the body through some impelling and active force (441/45/81).

To become a channel for the creative power of the universe, you must learn to listen to your intuition and to act on it at all times, even at the risk of going against patterns, expectations and belief systems (757/37/73).

Spontaneous channelling: the more you are willing to surrender to the energy within, the more power can flow through you (538/52/88).

By tuning-in to the intuition and allowing it to become the guiding force in our lives, we allow the conductor (the universal mind) to take its rightful place as the leader of the orchestra. Rather than losing our individual freedom, we will receive the support we need to effectively express our individuality, and we will, moreover, enjoy the experience of being part of a larger creative channel (1063/76).

If you can plug into and work with the energies of nature, instead of trying to overcome them or combat them, you will have plugged into an enormous pattern of power sources (700/70).

As people share or transmute this universal energy or consciousness to others, the stock of energy itself grows, giving strength to the Light (576/36/54).

The higher *the source of consciousness* (103/4) the higher will be *the sense of Light* (73/1).

Attuning yourself to the awareness that all things are energy gives a new perspective from which to grow (429/69).

Love is the essence in spiritual fire (155/11/65).

The strongest form of energy is love (158/14/68).

If one's purpose is love, if action is love nothing can be wrong, for then power will be gained for The Light (519/69).

Cosmic light force is to be shared equally and owned by all (222/24/42).

Spirit is the essence of consciousness, the energy of the universe that creates all things. Each one of us is part of that spirit - a divine entity. So the spirit is the higher self, the eternal being that lives within us (786/64/73).

The direction for one to go is with God who is energy (245/29/65).

Energy cannot move in a situation where two parts of yourself, the tyrant and the rebel, are doing battle, and you are not dropping into your intuition for guidance (667/37/64). [Note I refer to: *the tyrant - the subconscious brain* (127/19/37) and *the rebel - the conscious brain* (117/18/27).]

If we continually turn away from the internal us, at least whilst living in time and space, a form of "static energy" will be created which will arise and try and call us back and reground us (691/61).

If you can plug into and work with the energies of nature instead of trying to overcome then or combat them, you will have plugged into an enormous pattern of power sources (700/70).

The unconscious is somehow connected to fields of energy which all matter, organic and inorganic, possess (420/60).

Investigate energy, try and understand it, then use it, for it is to be found everywhere (355/31/85).

Energy on the move is not a physical heat, only a perception (248/23/68).

As we don't have an energy sense, the connection to the universe is not felt. However, we use the skin instead and thus experience a feeling of warmth, but only on the physical level (679/49).

Energy is information with a significance (200/20).

The higher the source of consciousness the higher will be the sense of light (325/37/55).

If a spiral represents "the way", it is also expressive of a powerful change of energy (349/79).

When you are willing to trust and follow your energy, it will lead you into relationships from which you have the most to learn. The stronger the attraction the stronger the mirror. So the energy will always lead you to the most intense learning situation (1036/19).

One's signature reveals the energy that is currently available (242/26/62).

[Note: this remark refers to the action (or lack thereof) of a pendulum which is held over the signature. As the flow of energy through the body rises, perhaps in doing Reiki, the signature subtly changes as does the action of the pendulum.]

A pendulum which swings when held above a person's signature is providing an appraisal of the energy within the soma (481/31/49).

117

The Light is the energy which keeps alive your life force, which is the Soul of Light which gives life to the form each of us is. Without the Soul of Light the form ceases to exist (737/17/71).

Banked-up energy will sooner or later find its own path out if it isn't released naturally. It cannot work properly for maximized health (557/17/53).

Energy, to be effective, must be directional and not free-floating (260/80).

The intuition will develop from an understanding of energy (262/28/82).

Each human being is a unique musical instrument which can be tuned in, tuned-up, and played in harmony with others. When people are in time, an automatic gathering of energy happens (715/76/85).

Are you out of tune with yourself and the world around, feeling flat, striking a sour note or a wrong chord (439/79)?

There is no secret to having a beautiful body. Simply trust yourself and follow your natural needs. Tune in and honour your intuition. Keep the energy moving by backing yourself up moment by moment. Most importantly love and nurture yourself now. You are beautiful (1039/13).

Kundalini power is a perfectly natural part of man's total existence. It involves transfering a low voltage power from automatic activities of the sympathetic nervous system to make it part of the cerebrospinal system, the conscious awareness (943/97).

When the Kundalini rises, personal radiance also rises (214/25/34).

Kundalini is the very force which removes illusion and allows the mind to see that which is reality. It is the very force that makes man realize that he has divine potential (687/57/166).

When the kundalini is repressed, the body will be lacking in vitality (307/37).

When the vast mass of stored up kundalini is released to travel along the spinal canal and strike the head centres, the reaction is tremendous - far superior to the reaction of sense perception (659/29).

The awakening of the kundalini purifies the seeker. It rids him of all his old impressions, blocks and impurities. Because these vary from person to person the process is unique for everyone (783/63/72).

Kundalini is the essence of Aum. When she is awakened, lives which had seemed commonplace and arid, unenjoyable and frustrated, become gay and flourishing, filled with sweetness, contentment and delight (745/25/79).

The Hindu chant *OM NAMA SHIVAYA* (60/6) is used to awaken the kundalini. Vibration number 60 is also the vibration of *Integration: the body and consciousness working in union* (240/60).

Apana is a negative force which flows from the navel to the anus. It is a form of "ida" and its downward flow not only eliminates bodily wastes, but also maintains kundalini activity in the generative organs (722/74/92).

Prana is a low voltage energy composing the body of the ki-subconscious energy within (347/32/77).

Without magnetism there would be no life force. *The human body is essentially an electromagnetic machine* (221/23/41). Every single cell in our bodies is an electrical unit with a magnetic field of its own.   (755/35/71)

Electromagnetism (71/8) is an intensity force that permeates the atomic structures of all objects, including the surrounding atmosphere. Being a natural force it has a rapport with the energy within the body.   (803/83)

Being out of harmony with the pulse of nature reduces the

119

amount of available electromagnetism (366/33/96).

The natural harmonies contribute to the preservation of the body through some impelling and active force (441/45/81).

We are all genetically tuned to receiving a different set of melodies from the magnetic symphony of the solar system (470/20).

The trouble with electromagnetic energy blocked within the body is that sooner or later it must escape somewhere, all too often resulting in bodily dysfunction (641/11/65).

Electromagnetism is the mystical water of life (185/14/95).

From breathing stems feeling; from feeling stems energy; from energy stems the pursuit of knowledge (425/47/65).

The meridians may be the threshold between pure energy and its first manifestation as microscopic matter (425/47/65).

The symbolic form of numerals in combination can represent an underlying energy (348/33/78).

The energy embodied within a single numeral, or combination of numerals, is an invisible force (366/33/96).

Spiritual Healing (82/1)

It is, of course, a matter of definition as to exactly what spiritual healing encompasses. So, let us see if we can get the answer from vibration number 82 - I think we can. We also find in this vibration:

cell regeneration	*energy harmony*
the *healing centre*	the *genius of nature*
the *universal source*	the *cure for cancer*

Cell regeneration is the body's ability to replace any, or all, diseased or dying cells (336/39/66). From this vibration one also learns that a *properly grounded person will be fit and well and able to access energy through the feet* (426/48/66). And to cap it all, still in the same vibration, we find *the Odic Force* (66/3) at one end of the health spectrum and at the other end, *the diseased body* (66/3).

Because we humans "walk" on the ground, we get the impression that we must be *in touch with the earth* (100/10). This is, of course, not so, because by far the largest majority of us insulate our feet from the earth with shoes.

We are all well aware of *the cold hands and feet in winter syndrome* (170/80). For some reason this seems to show up more in women than men. It is a sure sign of *inadequate grounding* (98/8). Just because men don't seem to suffer from cold hands and feet, it doesn't necessarily follow that they are *properly grounded* (98/8).

To return to vibration number 82, one also finds a *thyroid dysbalance* (82/1). *The thyroid gland* (82/1) is, of course, in the throat. In my experience, *an energy imbalance in the throat chakra* (161/17/71) is a far more frequent occurrence than is generally realized.

Medical testing of the thyroid seems to be regarded as absolute. Although this may be so, I believe that thyroid activity goes up and down just as blood pressure varies with the amount of exercise one takes, and that any such measured test, be it for thyroid or for blood pressure, only reflects a measurement at a certain point in time.

Blood pressure may vary with exercise or liquid intake, etc. - *the thyroid reacts in accordance with internal frustration which is itself a measurement of one's ability to vocally self-express* (501/51/6). This causes many things including *stomach cancer* (51/6), *heart disease* (51/6) and *sweaty hands* (42/6).

The chronic fatigue syndrome (134/17/44) can perhaps be similarly understood. However, here we find that it is in the same energy frequency as *The Light* (44/8). This is not a reference to daylight but to *metaphysical light* (82/1). So, here we have a direct pointer to *spiritual healing* (82/1). The polarities of vibration number 44 are, on the one hand, *lacking joy*, on the other hand, *wellbeing*. There has to be *an internal disbalance* (79/7) that can explain *the exterior condition* (115/16/25/7).

So, what does *internal frustration* (92/2) amount to, other than the *thymus underactivity* (92/2) and *without a sense of health* (92/2). Whenever there is anything not right in the being of any sort, there will invariably be associated thymus underactivity.

Just about every time, we come around to *banked-up energy* (69/6) which reflects on *kidney performance* (92/2). Reflect that number 6 is the home of the kidneys. It is very easy to test the relevant chakra. This is done with a pendulum or a simple divining rod. *Properly grounded individuals* (150/60/6) are rare indeed and it is so easy to correct.

The laying-on of hands (89/8) or Reiki is the way to achieve this, but do make sure that if you are treated by someone, it is by a *spiritual healer* (76/4) who has *a oneness with the Cosmos* (89/8) as well as with *The Ground of Being* (89/8).

I called this segment *spiritual healing* (82/1), so I must mention that *the power of God* (76/4) is the same vibration as for *a spiritual healer* (see above). Taken literally number 76 reads *social interaction* (79/7) and *harmony* (42/6), which is exactly what *healing* (38/2) is all about.

Every one of us has what is known as *free choice* (59/5). In other words one can believe all this or one can discard it all; it is always up to the individual. But the same vibration also covers *true mastery* (59/5). This becomes more significant when one realises that *accessing energy from the earth* (140/50/5) is also in the same vibration.

It is also worth noting that the very same vibration also contains:

• *a properly grounded individual* (140/50/5)

- *free-floating energy* (104/14/5).

So, *energy, to be effective, must be free-floating* (260/80). In other words, it is unwise to do what so many women seem to do - direct all their energy to *the sacral chakra* (57/3); or what many men do - direct all their energy to *the solar plexus chakra* (84/3).

It is no accident that under vibration number 260/80 one finds:

- *potential energy - universal energy*
- *the way to The Light - the energy door.*

The medical profession has clearly come up with some quite wonderful techniques, but as a body they have hardly got anywhere in the *understanding of what makes a person ill* (150/60). So, we come round again to the need for every being to be a *properly grounded individual* (150/60). It is only then that *spiritual healing* (82/1) becomes possible.

Having said this, from time to time there is talk of *quantum healing* (64/1). Again, it is no accident that this is in the same vibration as *spirituality* (64/1) or *the God power* (64/1).

It is worth noting the definition for *a symbol: a common mode of communication used separately, or in combination, to convey simple or complex concepts that impact on consciousness and thus produce energy* (631/64). In attuning students the Reiki Master uses three symbols *for accessing energy for the individual benefit* (196/16). Here, it is worth recalling that these numerals can all be read forwards or backwards, because of the divination that reads *the tremendous potential energy that lies within all symbols* (241/25/61).

No writing on spiritual healing would be complete without one more definition - *energy: a measure of the tremendous potential of one's developing consciousness to influence the mind* (402/42). This happens to be the vibration of *the search*

(42/6), *the source* (42/6), and *the answers* (42/6).

Whilst writing this, a caller came in named Elizabeth - not Liz, not Beth, just full-blown Elizabeth. She has three children and is divorced. A look at her Kabala shows:

E	L	I	Z	A	B	E	T	H
5	3	9	8	1	2	5	2	8
8	3	8	9	3	7	7	1	
2	2	8	3	1	5	8		
4	1	2	4	6	4			
5	3	6	1	1				
8	9	7	2					
8	7	9						
6	7							
4								

At her age 37, notice the number 93 which reads both:

- *energy availability,* and
- *the healing potential.*

This vibration occurs in both the line slanting down to the right from the letter Z and, where that line joins the next one, down in the same direction from the letter A. What is more, this occurs precisely on target for her present age. With three young children she is a typical "mum", but she does have a part-time job which gives her some satisfaction. However, she knows that there is more in life for her, and I am sure she will, in due course, become a very good spiritual healer. Notice too, the number 88 which leads up to her letter Z from the left. This reads as *a very strong channel.*

There is, I know, *tremendous talent* (62/8) out there in the population that is ideal for *spiritual teaching* (84/3). I can only hope that this work will encourage it to come forth. I know that Elizabeth, to whom I have referred, is in the group.

The Law of Karma

The Law of Karma (53) implies that the universe is an eternal moral order. (262/28/82)

Science tells us that the world is controlled by natural physical forces. Chance is said to preside over the casting and recasting of the cosmic weather. (571/31/58)

Karma says, that behind the apparently blind mechanical or physical forces, there is a principle of *cosmic intelligence* (87), a power, which controls the operations of nature and guides the destiny of mankind. (819/99)

Karma is regarded as a fundamental spiritual law (166/13/76).

Science has faith in the conservation of energy, the sum total of energy in the universe remaining constant, not an iota ever being lost. Any apparent change is regarded as being in the nature of a transformation of energy, where energy passes from one form to another. (1090/19)

Religion has faith in the conservation of the higher values of life - truth, beauty, goodness, freedom and honesty. The world is not regarded as a field of accidental forces blindly jostling at one another, but is considered to be ultimately determined by a supreme spiritual being. (1100/20)

We live in a world with an eternal moral order, says the law of karma. When there is any disturbance of the moral balance of the universe, the moral balance will vindicate itself by suitably reacting against the person causing the dysbalance. (891/81)

Any such person who disturbs the moral balance of the universe will suffer a considerable drop in his level of consciousness, which will bring in its trail other upheaval. First to be affected will be personal happiness or joy. (890/80)

The moral quality of any action, the intentions and motives, are major factors in proceeding events, in the causing of things that will eventuate in life and in nature. Moral qualities are not ineffective things, not just mental ideas. They are objective forces, albeit invisible, in life and nature

125

According to the law of karma, the invisible force which seems to control us from day to day, is not a supernatural external power with which we have no apparent organic connection. It is the outcome of various past individual or collective actions, for we are all, individually and collectively, the architects of our own virtue. In the past we contributed to the formation of that invisible force that is holding sway today. (1659/75)

What is known as *fate* (14/5) does not leave room for the creative freedom we undoubtedly all have, whereas the law of karma is perfectly compatible with it. (554/14/59)

Our actions, whether individual or collective, get us involved in a circle, and even if it is too late, it is difficult for us to get out of that circle. When we can rise above the law of karma, we attain liberation or salvation. (850/40)

The important spiritual principle in life is the principle of non-attachment. If we can practise non-attachment, we can go through the changing circumstances of life without suffering the adverse consequences of them. (891/81)

According to the law of karma, even though we have a kind of destiny, we also have a freedom. Destiny, properly understood, is not incompatible with our creative freedom. It is actually the outcome of this freedom. (830/20)

The bonds of karma are shattered when we become integrated with absolute spirit (305/35).

Talking of Symbols

Symbols are the storehouse of the energies of nature. Their use impacts on a person's higher consciousness, thereby raising his or her energy level. (618/69/78)

Symbols have extraordinary power in human consciousness. They are a material object representing something, often something immaterial, usually an idea or set of ideas. (663/33/69)

Symbols exist all around us. The swastika and hammer and sickle are symbols which elicit in one certain reactions - but how many people can define exactly what they stand for? And, depending upon one's values, one's reaction to each symbol will be positive or negative. (967/94)

Symbols are all around us, even in the more mundane area of brand names, like Coca Cola or BHP. A symbol can be a letter, figure, or a combination of letters or numbers used to represent an object or idea, as in chemistry or numerology.

(846/36/81)

Symbols represent a mental focus for the emotional reaction to the idea or set of ideas behind a particular symbol. Initially, they bypass consciousness and go straight to the emotions, the powerful and automatic reactions to subconsciously held values. However, with continuous usage, symbols can and do impact on the level of consciousness which begins to rise. (1339/43)

Symbols are thought by most people to be the opposite of ideas, thoughts, or concepts that are rationally and precisely defined, and intellectually held. As such, symbols lack intellectual clarity. Each can mean different things to many people. (901/91)

The impact of a symbols grows in magnitude with their continued usage (256/22/76).

The visualization or practical usage of symbols will unleash the incredible energies of nature that are hidden within (483/33/42).

The body image is the key to the symbolism of the body, the relationship of body and mind, and so sometimes the key to discovering meanings of illnesses, emotional needs that are being expressed in terms of sickness (825/15/87).

Symbolism supposes that cancer is a physical expression of fear and a sense of loss - so, to treat the cancer without curing the fear of growth, maturity and loss of ego, means that the fear will only manifest in some similar or new way. (893/83)

All symbols give visible form to the invisible forces of life, most especially the inner patterns and workings of the psyche, which determine the sequence of life as well as man's experience of the cosmos. (826/16/86)

Dream symbols are, for the most part, manifestations of a psyche that is beyond the conscious mind. Meaning and purposefulness operate in the whole of living nature and are not just a function of the mind. (770/50)

When the body and psyche have been symbolically identified, a purely mental solution or symbol will not be enough. A physical symbol, or symbolic action, may be required to counterbalance (offset) any damage. Where the problem is primarily intellectual (to do with the male conscious ego or animus), then a solution in the intellectual sphere is indicated. The same goes for the emotions and the anima. (1540/64)

Symbolism is the language of both nature and the universe. As truths about the cosmos are too vast to take in, the overall vision of reality can be digested by man, and therefore be of value to the individual, only when compressed into a symbol (913/94).

Symbols point outwards through time and space, beyond the confines of any individual symbol, however, concrete or abstract. Although they may be able to guide intuition and feeling beyond the limits of ego-consciousness to the broadest possible vision of reality for man, symbols are always, in the final analysis, inadequate. (1215/36)

"Aum" may be regarded as a symbol of the universe: past, present, and future. Repeating it as a mantra, either mentally or orally, is of vital importance in one's meditative approach to self-realization (743/23/77).

[Note: Numbers may themselves be used as a mantra in exactly the same manner:]

- Number 135, 1-3-5, not one hundred and thirty-five, will raise one's individual energy level in accordance with the number of times one silently chants 1-3-5 to oneself. It is the vibration for both the *opening of the Third Eye* (135/18/45), as well as *the life force of the Universe* (135/18/45).

Where there is a special name for a symbol, it may be said silently or even chanted as a mantra:

- *Dia-ko-Mio* is the symbolic key to accessing the Great Spirit, and thereby activating the power within each of us (447/442/87).
- *Sei-he-ki* is the symbolic key to accessing mental energy (208/28).
- *Hon-sha-ze-sho-nen* is the symbolic key for activating and transmitting one's distant healing powers (395/35).
- *Bay-la* is a very powerful symbol capable of being the catalyst to very powerful changes in one's life (383/23/32).
- *Tam-a-ra-sha* - is an enhancement of the intuitive understanding of spiritual awareness and spiritual consciousness (401/41).

[Note: this is one of the Kofutu symbols. It happens to look very like the female end of an electric extension chord. An obvious analogy indicates a receptivity to, and a channel for, spiritual energy.]

- *Zoh-va* - through this consciousness connection one can reach directly into the life or existence force of anyone or anything (532/55/82).

[Note: this Kofutu symbol has the very definite format of two people who have a very close heart connection.]

Symbols describe pictorially and vividly what is of greatest concern to man - his own inner being and its relationship to the universe around. Some symbols (snakes, bulls, trees) are taken directly from nature. They are used to describe the symbolic effect they have as they break into a man's psyche at moments of intense value and significance. Other symbols (dragons and Gods) erupt from the psyche.   (1496/56)

Symbolism was the traditional religious language of mankind, and most symbols can be traced back to their use in ritual. But ritual, as the creative expression of the psyche, reflects the pattern and structure of the psyche, and of life.

(876/66/84)

The religious establishments have often lost touch with their own symbolic roots. Religion is crumbling, chiefly because those entrusted to transmit it don't know what they are talking about.   (759/39)

Symbolism fulfilled the need to conceal sacred truths from the uninitiated and to offer a language for those qualified to understand it (541/55/91).

Numerals represent a complete symbolism, no doubt originally based on a mythology of the cosmos, society and man, but expressed in a shorthand or somewhat abstract form (612/63/72).

The spiral is a magical symbol intended to depict the mystical journey to the centre, where illumination, wisdom or insight will be found. Most people live horizontally, and only a few access the vertical type of life. The perfect motion is spiral. The vertical experience is for the overcomer, and forms a cross with the horizontal, ordinary human existence. Because the spiral is used to convert radio waves into electrical impulses, the capacity exists to move from one level to another, or from one vibration to another.   (2071/28)

The symbol of The Cross shows that a sacrifice of self is

necessary to cross over into the state of supraconsciousness. Because the vertical is linked with thinking and the circle with spirit, a special symbol combining the two represents the higher mental (spiritual) faculty of mankind. (696/66)

The Divided Circle represents the dualistic role of man who dwells in light and darkness (356/32/86).

The Circle is an indicator of activity and an energetic masculine personality (309/39).

The image of the Half Circle is intended to evoke the idea that man (symbolized as two half circles joined together) belongs partly to the lower infernal realm, and partly to the highest seat of God. (763/43/79)

In The Square all feelings and desires must be made straight and in the right relationship to each other, and united with each other. (521/53/71)

Odd Numbers represent the creative male principle and are related symbolically to the idea of unity, the union of opposites, because they cannot be divided by two. (636/69/96)

Even Numbers represent the duality and conflict of everyday ordinary existence. (391/31)

Finally, of course, pain can be imagined symbolically:

- overcoming the need for outside treatment,
- healing through white cells overcoming the problem,
- actively and aggressively (643/13/67).

Rejoice in the Rediscovery of Reiki

It is now history that a class of students studying divinity at the small Christian University asked of their professor, Dr Mikao Usui, "Sir, you say that Jesus healed, how did he heal"? It is now a matter of record that Dr Usui did not know the answer, but was sufficiently stimulated by the enquiry to set out on a long journey that was in the end to prove fortuitous.

Hoping to find the answer, Dr Usui decided to move to America where he was to study Christianity at a theological college near New York. However, the answer eluded him, and so he decided to move to China to learn Chinese, all in the hope of finding the answer. Again, he was to be unsuccessful.

Not to be outdone, Dr Usui decided to learn Sanskrit, an ancient language of the East. A lot of researching and travel led him eventually to a monastery, where he was to find some notes of a monk who assisted Buddha's healing. It is wonderful that they had been preserved, for here was the record of the symbols used to access healing energy. It was a miracle that Dr Usui was lucky enough to discover those notes.

So Dr Usui knew how to access energy, but he still did not have the power to heal. On advice he decided to go to a monastery, where he was to meditate for twenty-one days. On the 21st day, a beam of light appeared from heaven and struck Dr Usui, who then realised he had the power to heal.

Numerologically, albeit with the benefit of hindsight, it is possible to record:

- the name Mikao has a Motivation number 16.

Then embedded within vibration number 16, one finds the following very relevant divinations:

- *Unravelling the Reiki mystery* (142/16),
- *My stimulating discoveries* (115/16),
- *The perfection of consciousness* (133/16),
- *Climbing to the top of the mountain* (115/16),
- *The appearance of a beam of light from heaven* (178/16),
- *Gaining the power to heal* (115/16),
- *God sometimes moves in a mysterious way* (151/16).

Incredible? Maybe. However, Dr Usui had clearly obtained

the answers. He now knew how Buddha healed and perhaps, therefore, how Jesus healed.

Subsequently, it wasn't until the early 1980's that these secrets were passed on by a Japanese-American lady, Mrs Takata, who was the second in succession to be taught them. She passed the details onto a group of three ladies including her grand daughter Phyllis Furmuto who was to found the Reiki Alliance.

There is now a growing number of Reiki Master Teachers with knowledge of *the Hands-on Healing technique* (116/17/26) that was rediscovered by Dr Usui, and is now known as *the Reiki technique* (97/16).

The Reiki Master (71/8) literally has *the ability to pull energy out of the air* (171/18/81) using a series of three symbols, two of which are taught to students who study the second stage. My teaching incorporates additional symbols.

This is done in a series of four *energy attunements* (75/3) for the first stage, with one other to follow in the next stage. Unlike some Reiki Masters who teach over fifty students at one time, my own classes are always small and even face to face.

With small classes the teaching for both stages is done comfortably in just one day for each stage. I can only say from my own experience that the satisfaction which comes from observing the clear change in students in just the few minutes the attunements take has to be seen to be believed. Students tell that they have changed, and it is quite clear that they have.

During the four attunements, students become increasingly aware that they have acquired what may be termed *"hot healing hands"* (73/1). This comes about as a result of the Master having rejoined each student to his or her source, thereby letting *universal energy* (80/8) again flow through the

The Hidden Wisdom Within Numbers

body, *eliminating the energy blockages that cause so many attitudinal upsets and health problems* (330/60).

Reiki - Essential Wellbeing

There exists *One Supreme Being* (78) - the Absolute Infinite - a dynamic force that governs the world and universe. It is an unseen spiritual power that vibrates and all other powers fade into insignificance beside it. So, therefore, it is *Absolute.* (938/92)

The universal power is unfathomable, immeasurable and even incomprehensible to man. And yet, it is there and available to be used by every single being. It has become known as Reiki. (675/45/63)

Reiki is neither electricity, a wireless wave, or an X-ray. Because it comes from the Great Spirit, it can penetrate even a thick windjammer or a doona. (585/45/54)

Reiki is an absolutely harmless and safe treatment. It certainly does not destroy delicate tissues or nerves. Being a universal wave, everything that has life benefits when treated. (672/42/69)

Reiki should be applied and used daily as a prevention. God's plan provided us with everything. We have hands to use the energy to apply and heal, to retain physical health and mental balance, to free ourselves from ignorance, and to live in an enlightened world. (1011/12)

With discipline and therefore daily application the body will respond, and all we wish and desire to attain in this world is then within reach. Health, happiness and the road to longevity, which we all seek, can be called perfection. (921/93)

Being a universal force from the Great Divine Spirit, Reiki belongs to all who seek and desire to learn the art of healing. It knows no colour, nor creed, neither old nor young. It will find its way when the student is ready to accept. He or she is

134

shown the way. Initiation is a sacred ceremony and the contact is made. Because we are associating with the Divine Spirit, there is no error nor should we doubt. (1551/66)

After Reiki initiation, the hands radiate vibrations when applied to the ailing part. It relieves pain, stops the blood from an open wound, produces good sleep. Your hands are ready to heal acute and chronic diseases both in human beings and all living things. (1022/14)

In acute cases only a few minutes application is necessary. In chronic cases, the first step is to find the cause and effect. The patient should only loosen tight clothing and does not have to undress completely. (773/53/71)

During the treatment trust in your hands. Listen to vibrations or reactions. It registers pain in the healer's fingertips and palm. If deep and chronic, it will throb a deep pain, and if acute, the pain is a shallow tingle. (937/91)

As soon as the body responds to a Reiki treatment, the acute ailment disappears but the cause remains. Dig into the cause daily and with each treatment. An improvement will be seen. If necessary talk with a Reiki Master to aid in understanding the cause. (904/94)

With experience, which comes through discipline in the use of Reiki, the hands become more and more sensitive and are able to determine the cause and to detect the slightest congestion within, whether physical or mental, acute or chronic. Reiki will adjust the body to normal. (1102/22)

Great change can take place in the body sometimes in less than a week, though it can occasionally take longer. Then all internal organs or glands will begin to function with much more vigour and rhythm. Reiki achieves this and much more. (907/97)

Following this, the digestive juices put out normal flow, the congested nerves slacken, the adhesions break away, the lazy colon gets organized, the faecal matter drops from the walls of the intestines, the gases eliminate, and many fears of accumulated toxins find their way out through the pores.

(1094/14)

Then bowel action increases and takes on a dark and strong odour, and the urine becomes dark. This is the manifestation of a big general overhaul of the intestinal organs taking place. With such good cleansing, the body becomes active once more. The numbed nerves regain a sense of feeling, appetite increases, sound sleep becomes natural, the eyes sparkle, and the skin glows.

(1346/41)

With new blood and good circulation, it is possible to rejuvenate five to ten years (417/48/57).

Venturing into Reiki II and Beyond

Reiki was reborn when Dr Usui had the good fortune to discover drawings of the symbols that Buddha had used for Hands-On Healing. Apparently these had been carefully written down by a monk who obviously assisted in the healings.

I suggest it is no coincidence that numerologically the divination which reads, *venturing into Reiki* (105/15/6), has the same vibratory frequency as the divination which reads, *an adventure into symbolism* (105/15/6). After all, symbols are the language of nature.

In Reiki II, *the energy that is hidden within symbols* (177/87/15/6) is unlocked and students are introduced to six powerful symbols.

Those who happened to live in wartime England will surely recall the famous Churchillean "V" for Victory symbol, which is made with the first and second finger of either hand. The energy generated was enormous and the people became totally dedicated, totally determined to win the war.

136

Certainly, it was all in peoples' minds, and to understand symbols one must first appreciate the power of the mind. A definition for the mind could well read, *The Mind - the energy generator* (141/51/15/6).

Every time so far, we seem to return to vibration number 15/6. So it is reasonable, indeed logical, to also find under this vibration:

- energy moving vertically (123/33/15/6),
- the rich and prosperous guru within me (177/87/15/6),
- the Master of the Universe (105/15/6).

So, all this comes to the student through *the understanding of symbols* (104/14/5). It is not inconsequential that the following divinations occur under this different vibration:

- spiritual understanding (104/14/5),
- the magnet that draws God to you (113/23/14/5),
- the Higher Self; the soul (104/14/4).

Thus through the Reiki II experience which includes a brief venture into Kofutu symbols, one's vertical development is appreciably accentuated. All students know much more about themselves, and in particular about *the powerful energy accessible through the mind* (212/23/32/5).

After studying Reiki II, the door would be open for you to consider teaching. *The spiritual experience* (103/13) that teaching brings is just great.

Understanding the Chakras

The basal chakra (47/2) deals with issues of earth-plane grounding and understanding of the physical dimension. It governs adrenal responses of flight or fight as well as the kidneys, should there be any feeling of sluggishness or lack of energy.   (929/29)

It is important to have the basal chakra, which channels *the energy of the human will* (123/15/33), balanced with the higher chakras of Divine vibration. This has the effect of making you a much easier person to get to know or to live with.   (881/71/89)

It is important to realize that *no one can have total health when they have massed or banked-up energy at their basal/sacral chakra centres* (374/14/32). *It is essential to be able to access the Earth's energy through one's feet and legs up to the basal chakra and beyond* (390/30), and vice versa, to similarly release surplus energy down to the ground. It is thus so necessary to balance the basal chakra.   (1327/49)

The sacral chakra (57/3) governs the physical and emotional issues of creativity and sensuality. When the chakra is balanced, a much grander feeling of the total merging and creative potential of the male and female occurs.   (804/84)

When balanced *the second chakra* (63/9) becomes the way of confronting any fear of being uncreative, unproductive. This puts one in touch with the fundamental understanding that *the human body is basically an aggregate of universal particles that the Higher Self has sculpted to experience a physical existence and truly fulfil its purpose for that lifetime* (717/78/87).   (1371/48)

It becomes clear that the Higher Self is never dispersed, but is indeed the composer of the particles and of the symphony of life (523/55/73). *Through the second chakra the composer and the composed become one for a time, yet it is possible to have a distinction between the two* (508/58).   (1031/14)

It is also important to balance *the solar plexus chakra* (84/3). *The third chakra governs our attitudes towards personal power and sensitivity and the ego* (361/37/91). The ego is connected to the fear of losing something, or some part of oneself or someone. Out of the fear springs the need to manipulate, bully, or in some other way control the people in one's life. *Relationships that cause emotional upset are always about personal power and the ego in relation to one's sensitivities* (451/46/91). (1761/87)

When one becomes attuned in the third chakra, one likes oneself better, feels more self-confident, and thus more *capable of breaking any restrictive bonds of the negative ego* (248/23/68). Any fat that one holds in that area begins to disappear, because *fat is anger withheld and blocked* (125/17/35). (1008/18)

The balancing of the third chakra will bathe in light the pancreas, which governs the actions of the liver, spleen, gall bladder and stomach. It contributes to the calming and relaxation of the nervous system. *How one abuses, misuses, or doesn't use one's personal power is directly related to the balance of the third chakra* (414/45/54). (1200/30)

When the third chakra is recognized by the conscious mind as healthy, it is reinforced as to the role it plays, not only in one's physical life, but in one's emotional life as well. The effect can be startling. (796/76)

Once the third chakra is balanced, the stomach, liver, gallbladder, and spleen are relaxed and vibrating at a more even frequency. Any problems of egotism are reduced.

(625/67/85)

To be more aware of the value of the chakra system is to be more aware of one's internal power (346/31/76). *To be more aware of the internal power is to understand the potential for external power* (359/89). *One can create whatever one wants on the exterior by recognizing what power is hidden in the interior* (456/42/96). (1161/27)

In balancing *the heart chakra* (64/1), one is stimulating it to be more effective in governing the love feelings which harmonize the immune and endocrine systems. *When there is love the whole body is affected* (185/14/95). (828/18/81)

Until one can love oneself one has no power, and the love of others is not possible (308/38). The self-confidence derived once the heart chakra is open will carry a subtle vibration that will be felt by all those around. *We receive from others what we have seen and created in ourselves - an inner security creates security in others* (448/43/88).   (1265/32)

The throat chakra (67/4) is the centre through which we communicate and express ourselves. *The fifth chakra* (70/7) is the centre through which we formulate judgements of others. It also governs the organs that translate air into expression: the lungs vocal chords and bronchial tubes.   (1053/18)

We tend to cling to hate or anger just as an anchor, for feelings anchor us. *Anger gives us a dramatic role, fires us up, creates energy, defines a relationship* (325/37/55). It can even anchor us with the unconscious fear of what may fill the gap if we get rid of it! But *when we are able to let anger go, relief floods in, love flows in, and the chakras become better balanced* (318/39/48).   (1331/44)

Love is the glue that holds everything together. It is the channel of communication, and it expresses itself also through the fifth chakra (552/12/57). *The judgement we made that was previously rejected by others will now be understood and welcomed, because the new energy behind it is positive* (481/31/49).   (1099/19)

Remember that a blockage in the fifth chakra may well be caused by a fear of speaking the truth. *To constantly attempt to please others, whilst sacrificing your own true expression, can develop into a deep frustration of communications* (546/51/96).   (889/79)

The fourth or heart chakra is related to the fifth or throat chakra which in turn relates to the third or solar plexus chakra (504/54). This alignment is always there, though we may not be aware of it. It is only through conscious acknowledgment, only through deliberate recognition of the natural harmony, that we derive its strength. We are what we are conscious of. (1420/52)

The sixth chakra (65/2) is located between the two eyebrows above the nose. This, *the third eye chakra (88/7)*, governs the way we present ourselves to the world. It externalizes as the pituitary gland. It governs much of the lower brain and nervous system. Through it all our incoming and outgoing thoughts and visions are controlled. It is the centre of the eye of awareness. (1399/49)

The energy in the brow chakra (130/40) can be used in any way we wish. Its internal and external manifestation relates entirely to one's choice of thoughts. *Through the third eye we can harness, orchestrate, and expand the God-given energy within (381/21/39).* (956/92)

The seventh chakra (69/6), known as *the Crown chakra (67/4)*, has the highest vibrational frequency of all. It is *the centre for the ultimate in Divine integration (219/39)*. The higher one goes the further one can see, both spiritually and physically. (915/96)

Problems that previously loomed gigantic now seem silly, not because they are smaller but because we are bigger than they are. From this vantage point it is easier to see how *dark emotions - fear, depression, hatred, and so on - sap our energy and ultimately result in illness (366/33/96)*. But now anger will give way to understanding, hate will give way to love, and possessiveness to freedom. Once this has happened the chakras are balanced. (1596/66)

When the crown chakra is balanced one is resonating in total alignment with the God force within (392/32).

The white light that is frequently mentioned represents the infusion of all emotional frequencies. These become perfectly realized when the chakras are balanced (664/34/61).

The word *love* (18/9) is used and abused by most of us. Where a spiritual search is taking place, it is a word evoked more often than any other. *The need for ways to freely give and receive love is basically what motivates spiritual curiosity* (397/37). *Love flows when the chakras are balanced* (141/15/51). Learning the Reiki technique is a very good way to balance the chakras and to raise the kundalini.   (1403/53)

The Solar Plexus (60/6)

The powers and activities of the Solar Plexus or the Abdominal Brain (76/4) are situated in the abdomen, as the name indicates. Some of its filaments accompany the branches of the aorta (the great artery) and go to the stomach, intestines, spleen, pancreas, liver and certain other organs, but not to the lungs. It is situated in the upper part of the abdomen, behind the stomach, in front of the aorta and the pillars of the diaphragm.   (1549/64)

The Solar Plexus is the network of nerve fibres of *the great sympathetic nervous system* (121/13/31). It is composed of grey and white nervous substance, or brain matter. It receives and distributes nerve impulses to all of the abdominal organs, and supplies the organs of nutrition, assimilation, and distribution, with their nervous energy.   (1279/37)

The *Solar Plexus* performs most of the important offices in the vegetative life of the body, or being. It is the great powerhouse of the physical life energy, and bodily functions cannot be performed without it.   (874/82)

The Solar Plexus got its name for three reasons. Firstly, its central position; secondly its filaments extend in all directions to the important abdominal organs, like the rays of the sun; thirdly, it is recognized as being the powerhouse and great reservoir of *life force*, just as the sun is the great reservoir of material energy in the solar system.   (1236/39)

The Sympathetic Nervous System, over which the Solar Plexus presides, regulates and energizes the important functions of the organs upon which physical life depends, and by which it is sustained. (805/85)

The sympathetic system is quite distinct from the cerebrospinal system. It is known as the system of vegetative existence, because it presides over the processes of nutrition and growth in contradistinction to *the Cerebrospinal Nervous System* (135/18/45), which presides over distinctly animal faculties such as sensation, motion and intellect. (1308/48)

The sympathetic system controls the so-called automatic mechanisms of the body - the rhythmical beating of the heart, contraction and dilation of the arteries, the peristaltic action of the gastrointestinal tract, the contraction of smooth muscles, and the control and secretion of various glands. (1115/26)

The term "abdominal brain" conveys the idea that the Solar Plexus is endowed with the high powers and phenomena of a great nervous centre which can organise, multiply, and diminish forces or energy. (813/84/93)

[Note: The Abdominal Brain is found fully formed and perfect in the human embryo at the stage at which the skull brain of a developing unborn child is merely a pulpy mass of substance, incapable of performing any function whatsoever.]

The Solar Plexus is the seat of *the emotional nature of man* (103/13/4), as in reality it performs the part popularly held to be played by *the heart* (40/4). Just as *the heart and throat chakras have an interlocking functional relationship* (300/30) so do the navel and heart chakras. *All emotional states react both upon the internal organs as well as the outer avenues of expression - the throat, the arms, and the feet* (468/18/45). *The emotions work physiological changes in all organs, both internal and external* (330/60). (1733/86)

143

The close relationship of emotional feeling and the physical organs, regulated and supplied with energy by the sympathetic nervous system and not by the cerebrospinal system, shows us that *the seat of the emotions is within the great abdominal brain* (246/21/66), sometimes known as *God's own Plexus* (59/5). *The abdominal brain, or solar plexus, is the centre of life and life action* (284/14/21). (1351/46)

If we wish to regulate, control and direct our emotional nature, we must begin at the seat and centre thereof - the solar plexus. The strong men of our society have exercised emotional control to a great extent; lack of control is generally held to be a mark of weak character or flabby will. Control is generally effected by a very deliberate holding back, restraining or controlling an action which naturally tends to follow the rise of emotional feeling. (1800/90)

The most effective way for controlling emotional feeling is by way of awakening and controlling the solar plexus (451/46/91). The cerebrospinal nervous system (the parasympathetic nervous system) is *the seat of objective reactions* (114/15/24), and is directly linked with the sympathetic nervous system. Here the control is by the solar plexus, *the seat of subjective feelings and vital processes* (179/89). (1431/54)

The two nervous systems are interconnected by many delicate nervous filaments. Through these pass the messages which, on the one hand, cause the physical states to arouse the mental states; and, on the other hand, the messages causing the mental states, or ideas or reactions, to arouse physical states. (1043/17)

On the one hand we have the phenomenon of the disturbed liver, stomach, bowels, spleen, glands, and sexual organism, arousing corresponding ideas in the mind; and, on the other hand, we have the phenomenon of ideas held in the mind arousing activity of physical organs - the spleen, heart and sexual organism. If there were no such connecting links or nerves between the two nervous systems and their respective brains, the body and mind would act independently of each other. Such a dissolution of partnership would amount to the *severing of the silver chord.* (2285/44)

The interchange of messages and orders from one system to the other is, for the most part, performed unconsciously or instinctively by the nervous mechanism of the individual, who is neither aware of the process, nor does he consciously will its performance. It is however possible and practical to send appropriate messages from the cerebrum or *thinking brain* (73/1) to the solar plexus or *feeling brain* (66/3). (1634/77)

The cerebrum is far more influenced by the solar plexus than is generally realized. Nevertheless an individual can exert a tremendous influence over the latter more than most people realize. *When someone knowingly concentrates and uses his will, a tremendous power can be exerted by the cerebrum* (406/46). It is actually able to dominate to a great extent, and the solar plexus may be easily trained to accept its suggestions, its demands, its commands. (1654/79)

The reverse process is achieved once the dormant consciousness of the solar plexus is aroused. One must appreciate that *the instinctive mind of the solar plexus, or subconsciousness, is never asleep at the switch* (339/69), for it is always on the job to such an extent that it is practically dead to all the world other than that job. It is actually a most faithful and tireless worker especially once its mechanics are understood. (1539/63)

When someone is very wrapped-up in his work or hobby and practically unconscious of what else is going on around, quite an effort is sometimes needed to get such a person's attention. In the case of the solar plexus, arousal is achieved by concentrating one's directive thoughts on the pit of the stomach, which is where the solar plexus lies.   (1340/44)

You achieve the arousal of the solar plexus by either holding the required mental attitude, or by sending the thought to it (500/50). You do well to actually speak the words softly, thereby greatly aiding you in forming the clear thought which you wish to send to the instinctive mind. You should even try and regard yourself as addressing another individual. The more earnestly you carry out this idea, the more effective will be your results.   (1747/82)

The idea of talking to the solar plexus is not a mere fanciful notion. This is called autosuggestion (50/5). It goes far further than ordinary *autosuggestion*, because it establishes effective contact between two minds and two brains, even though they belong to the same individual.   (1022/14)

Having become acquainted with your solar plexus, and it with you - having established mutual harmony, confidence, and coordinated effort - you may proceed to give more definite and specific directions and suggestions. Always try to keep in mind the idea that you are really talking to another individual entity, and proceed to explain matters and to point out means and ways of action, just as you would when talking with another person.   (1615/76)

In explaining to the instinctive mind, the reason why certain emotional states or feeling are desirable or undesirable, advantageous or disadvantageous, you will find that it will willingly cooperate with you in repressing and restricting, or else in stimulating and encouraging, any emotional state to which you draw its attention.   (1337/41)

Here are some practical examples:

(for stimulation)	**(for restraint)**
the feeling of courage	the feeling of poverty
the feeling of involvement	the feeling of inadequacy

146

the feeling of confidence   the feeling of gloom or despair

The solar plexus will aid you in inhibiting the rise of anger (267/24/87), for anger and fear are the two great harmful emotional feelings, the first destroying by burning up and the second destroying by freezing up.   (866/56/83)

The solar plexus may be called upon for aid in stimulating the action of any physical organ which may have fallen into a habit of inactivity (547/52/97), albeit perhaps because of lack of proper treatment or ill-usage. It will restore normal and healthy functioning in any physical organ that has become affected for whatever reason.   (1252/37)

The instinctive mind will commence the fight against diseased conditions, or inactive functioning (412/43/52). When it doesn't receive proper cooperation from the cerebrum or thinking mind, it will simply do the best it can under the circumstance prevailing. Real, lasting results only come through active cooperation between the two minds. When it does find such cooperation in the matter of perfect organic functioning and improved physical condition, it responds willingly and even eagerly.   (2026/28)

In giving the instinctive mind the proper information, instructions, and directions in the matter of the restoration of physical health and proper functioning of the organs, always bear in mind the fact that the solar plexus understands its business and you do not have to tell it how to proceed to secure the results from the organs in its care. Being, as it is, God's own Plexus, it is a most wonderful maintenance establishment - after all God is better served when your being is in good condition.   (1945/19)

If you expect the solar plexus to do its share, you must be prepared to do yours. You must not and cannot expect to lie down at your end of the job, and have the solar plexus keeping busy at its end. If it finds you falling short, it will be apt to do the same. *Playing fair in securing health and strength requires the two minds or brains to be in full active partnership* (469/19). (1382/141)

The solar plexus must not be burdened with contrary emotions, or when food of the wrong sort, often improperly prepared and too much in quantity, is supplied. Also, the daily supportive liquid intake is important. (873/63/81)

The solar plexus is the source of vital force and physical energy - the great storehouse thereof, as well as its generator (465/15/42). If called upon for an increased supply for a good reason it will respond. You know what all this is about when you see this force manifesting within yourself, and expressing itself in your actions. (1248/33)

This vital force, an essential part of each of us, amounts to a reservoir of energy, enthusiasm, courage, animation. Numerologically, vibration 19 is *the vibration of Universal energy* (145/19/55). It is also *the Law of Thought as Destiny* (109/19), but sometimes it equally well represents the person who is *emotionally so very insecure* (127/19/37). Those lacking in energy will be spiritless, those possessing it will be spirited. We are all well aware of electricity. *Universal energy, though not electricity, has a current which is not dissimilar* (339/69). (1878/96)

The Reiki Technique is an excellent way to access Universal energy (265/22/85). And vibration 22, from which we learn this, also represents *The Great Divine Spirit* (112/13/22), as well as *the source of great contentment hidden within one* (211/22/31). (840/30)

Psychic powers are another phase of power inherent in the solar plexus. *Psychic power* (72/9) is that peculiar force, power, or energy which, when manifested by an individual, could be termed personal magnetism or even mind power. It is actually *thought transference* (92/9), for *all directive thoughts of man take upon themselves an individual physical form as they flow from one mind or brain to others* (504/54).

(1569/66)

The mental currents that constitute *psychic thinking* (87/6) are the mental vibrations of the directive thinking. They originate in the solar plexus in precisely the same way as one obtains vital force or physical energy from it.   (909/99)

The magnetic frequency of the solar plexus corresponds to the magnetic frequency of the earth (396/36).

Your Mind (47/2)

An understanding of *the mind* (37/1) requires knowledge of *the brain's potential* (82/1). Perhaps this is best illustrated by the divination which reads, *regenerative powers in the human body may be safely and intelligently harnessed by the conscious self within* (442/82/1).

Next, from vibration number 59 we learn that *when an individual is in contact with the universal mind through the subconscious, the fission of atoms within produces abounding energy* (572/32/59). And where do we find *abounding energy* (82/1)? Now this is particularly significant, for we also find *cell regeneration* (82/1) in the same vibration.

It has to be appreciated that the brain is considered to be composed of the same atoms that make up the rest of nature, and that the *disciplined focusing of the conscious mind on its interrelationship with the subconscious brain or universal mind causes a fission of atoms of which the brain consists, and thereby produces tremendous potential energy* (904/94). The effect is achieved rather as with the atomic bomb.

I suggest it is no coincidence that the same vibration is *the source of energy* (94), *the grounding chakra* (94), and *personal maximisation* (94).

Travelling further through the vibrations one finds *the*

conscious mind is just "the emergent apex", the top level of an enormous and sustaining subconscious (367/96). Perhaps this is why we also find *touching infinity* (97) in the same vibration.

The key to all this is *synchronicity* (76), for under this vibration we are told *the energy potential of the brain is generated by fission of the atoms of the brain once the mind is focussed* (438/78). Grouped here we also find *a divine elixir* (78), *pulsating energy* (78), and *spiritual welfare* (78).

Right from the outset I stated that vibration number 4 represented *the human mind* (58/4), and to date nothing has arisen to make me change my thinking, adding the proviso that I found that it is possible to rotate the number layout. Clearly the human mind is very dynamic and obviously affects the entire body, so it is not unreasonable to find clues to it coming up in other vibrations as we have found above.

Now we must turn our attention to *the universal mind, the source of all energy* (178/88/16), where we also find *the energies of nature* (88/16). It is appropriate to note that *the self-help technique of Reiki is a unique way of getting in touch with the life force energy, and of promoting your own healing and wholing, of maintaining positive wellness and of naturally opening yourself to a higher consciousness* (1015/16).

To have *the mind* and *the belly* in the same vibration number 37/1 has more logic to it than perhaps one appreciates. In common usage, the term *the mind* is regarded as referring to the activity of the conscious brain, which is of course in the head. Now, the somewhat vague term *the belly* refers to the area where the subconscious brain, the subconscious mind, is situated.

Two definitions are appropriate:

- *The Mind: the organized totality of psychological processes that enables the individual to interact with his environment* (502/52).

- *The Brain and its inherent capacity (the psyche) is a bridge between the genetic, vegetative world and the cosmic, physical world* (511/52/61).

Now number 52 is also the vibration for *the hand of Divine intelligence* (142/16/52) which I believe identifies the potential of the link between the two minds, the two brains.

And in number 52/7 we find *the intellect*. So, perhaps a definition for this is similarly appropriate. It would read, *The Intellect: the cognitive processes of thinking, relating and judging* (301/31). This has moved us into the vibration where we get the definition of "grounding", see page number 204. To cap it all number 31 is also the vibration for *the mysteries of consciousness* (121/13/31), which I guess just about sums up the state of our understanding of the interrelationship of mind, brain, and intellect.

I started with number 37/1 in reference to the mind, so I must finish with it. So look at these divinations:

- *the power penetrating the universe is much more than what shines through* (316/37/46)

- *so many people live with the lid on - cribbed, cabined, and confined in the human body, and bound by earthly materialistic thinking, when there are infinite levels of thought, intuition, and spiritual awakenings there for the asking* (937/37)

- *the mind cannot find perfect repose anywhere except in God. When you meet God you find everything and the mind becomes steady. Then, even if you try, it doesn't move. It is actually the restlessness of the mind that has never been satisfied by temporary stillness, which has set you on the search for truth and peace* (1216/37).

151

Chapter 5

Physical Healing Follows the Path of Spiritual Energy

Health (27/9) or Disease (26/8)

It is characteristic of illness that it is accompanied by changes in our state of consciousness. Even a simple headache or an attack of gout entails *a disturbance of consciousness* (106/16) and we feel unwell. (693/63)

It is in the nature of being ill that we become conscious of organic processes which normally pass unnoticed. *The state of well-being* (82/1) is characterized by *a total awareness of what is happening in our organs* (201/21), so that we become aware of their existence only when their function is disturbed.

(1130/23)

The processes of consciousness involve the presence of an astral body and an ego, and have as a natural consequence the processes of *physical breakdown* (80/8) and ultimately of death. (627/69/87)

When the nerve-sense processes become too dominant, they begin to encroach on the rest of the body-mind, where they manifest as *an abnormal state of consciousness* (109/19). This then affects various areas in the form of simple discomfort, pain or cramps, etc. (936/99)

The body-mind has a tendency either as a whole or in an isolated organ to develop too much head, and *the processes of consciousness and disintegration are intensified at the expense of those of growth and regeneration* (486/36/45). (863/53/89)

Thus we receive the fruit of the tree of consciousness and lose that of the tree of life. *Illness appears as a displacement of the etheric or astral forces, or a preponderance of one over the other* (424/46/64).   (764/44/71)

As long as the abnormal action of the astral and the ego affect the etheric body alone, one remains in the functional sphere (418/49/58), but if the abnormal action is sufficiently prolonged it can affect the physical body, stamping it like a seal on wax, causing physical effects.   (996/96)

It is possible that *the etheric body* (77/5) is sufficiently strong to compensate the action of *the astral and the ego* (75/3). So, the illness does not manifest itself on the functional level but remains latent.   (706/76)

It is only when a certain threshold is reached that the etheric body is no longer capable of renewing harmony and the illness becomes manifest (593/53).

So health is a precarious equilibrium that must be constantly renewed. *The great fomenter of troubles is the astral body and the greater healer is the etheric body* (321/33/51). This is not surprising when one recalls that the astral body is the bearer of one's instincts, passions and impulses.   (1068/15)

It so happens that man, within whom part of the etheric force has been diverted from the metabolic systems to be placed at *the service of self-expression* (132/15/42), is much more vulnerable than less evolved creatures, in which the etheric forces remain available for regeneration.   (1053/18)

It can happen that etheric forces become free and remain unutilized because the ego is not strong enough to metamorphose them into self-expressive force. *Unused etheric forces have the tendency to act on their own account, causing oliferation, abnormal vegetative processes, or tumour formation* (569/29). This circumstance is accompanied by a diminution of consciousness, as well as a certain degree of clouding of the mind. (1654/79)

Premature abstraction of etheric forces often results from *too early formal scholastic teaching* (147/12/57), which entails intellectual development before the necessary etheric forces have become free. (768/48/75)

The abstraction of etheric force is made at the expense of health (254/29/74).

When the forces of the astral body are insufficient for breaking down the foodstuffs and for the removal from them of their innate etheric forces, incompletely changed foodstuffs remain from this process and then become *a medium for pathological intestinal flora and fermentation* (243/27/63), and abdominal distension occurs. (1274/32)

Should the astral forces descend too forcefully, processes which normally take place at the level of the lungs - the liberation of carbon dioxide - occur at the level of the stomach or even the intestines, causing gas to collect in the stomach or intestine, giving rise to abdominal distension once again (1139/23).

Symptoms relating to the psyche are no less important than those relating to the physical body (371/11/38). The classification into mental and physical is somewhat schematic and really only relates to the predominant symptom among those observed. (904/94)

Every disease is accompanied by modifications of consciousness (253/28/73) and *no so-called mental illness exists which is not accompanied by physical changes* (294/24). *The body-mind is the instrument of the astral/ego complex* (224/26/44). (781/61/79)

The Matter of Stress

Stress touches the lives of everyone, and the *hectic pace of modern living* (143/17/53) means that nobody escapes. Stress is such a common part of our day that we hardly notice it any more. From the moment we awake, there are so many things to be done, to achieve, deadlines to meet, problems to solve. The pressures can quietly build without our noticing.

(1271/38)

Stress can usefully be thought of as *an unresolved inability* (100/10) to regain the capacity to adjust to *an imposed situation* (80/8). (420/60)

Most stresses do not lie in specific situations, but in an individual's capacity to deal with a situation. It is important to recognize that, as stress involves an individual's ability to deal with a situation, any development which impairs *the ability to adjust* (70/7) is effectively *a stress from within* (83/2). (1072/19)

Stress afflicts every organ of the body, causing a wide range of *seemingly unrelated symptoms* (119/29), *general ill health* (77/5), and a *lack of normal energy and vitality* (139/49/13). This returns our thinking to *energy* (40/4), or to *universal energy* (80/8). (865/55/82)

Stress is not necessarily the opposite situation from that most enjoyed, but *the loss of opportunity to engage in previously enjoyable pursuits is very stressful* (349/79), particularly if it occurs suddenly. (773/53/71)

Stress is a normal part of life (112/13/22). Some major life crises cannot be avoided, such as the death of a close relative or friend, personal injury, crimes, redundancy. *Even pleasant events can create stressful pressures* (172/19/82), such as getting married, or the arrival of a new baby. These events have a major impact on all lives and it often takes a while before the after-effects subside. (1339/43)

One of the main signs of stress is a *change in behaviour or emotion* (143/17/53). A person may start drinking more, or begin to smoke, or even take work problems home. Emotionally a person may begin to feel irritable, finding it difficult to relax and *feeling frustrated* (82/1), fed up, or *less confident* (55/1). (1180/28/10)

Stress does not need to be unpleasant, and indeed *a certain level of stress is necessary to maintain alertness and protect the body from injury* (352/37/82). (509/59)

The body responds to stress by mobilising *a defensive system* (67/4) involving *the pituitary and adrenal glands* (125/17/35). (418/49/58)

Should the adaptive system deteriorate, what follows is an illness with *tissue damage* (43/7), and perhaps *emotional breakdown* (80/8) too. (456/42/96)

Anger is a stress response, identical to fear (166/13/76). It is *the "fight or flight" syndrome* (141/15/51), the body's arousal for action in the face of a threat. (519/69)

Suppressing anger is not healthy (141/15/51). It is thought that *long term held-in anger* (102/12) can lead to a longer term raised blood pressure, ulcers and migraines. *Insomnia* (40/4), *depression* (52/7), *alcoholism* (44/8), and both *over-eating* (53/8) and *anorexia* (42/6) are all associated with *suppressed anger* (70/7). Even breast cancer patients are considered to have *an anger problem* (69/6), as most of them bottle up their feelings. (1276/34)

Musculoskeletal effects of stress (104/14)

Back pain, joint pain and stiffness, tired joints - arms and legs, headaches, migraine, twitching, cramps.

Mind/Psychological effects of stress (147/12/57)

Not coping, irritable, depression, personality change, unexplained or disproportionate anger, inability to concentrate, poor memory, fears/phobias, low self-esteem, inferiority complex, nightmares, frustration.

Sexual organs affected by stress (110/20)

Premenstrual syndrome, menopausal symptoms, hormonal imbalances, impotence, frigidity.

Gastrointestinal tract effects of stress (127/19/37)

Increased secretion of hydrochloric acid in the stomach, constipation/diarrhoea, wind/flatulence/burping, bloating, indigestion, nausea, vomiting, heartburn, burning sensation, stomach/abdominal pain, knot in the stomach, not hungry/eat all the time, allergies, loss of weight, increased weight.

Nervous system effects of stress (114/15/25)

Insomnia, tired all the time, unable to relax, lack of vitality/energy.

Cardiovascular system effects of stress (143/17/53)

Increased heart rate maintained for too long, heart pain/angina, palpitations, arhythmias, high blood pressure, chest pain/tightness, can precipitate narrow blood vessels, blood clots, high cholesterol levels.

Endocrine system effects of stress (132/15/42)

Hypoglycaemia, low thyroid function - depression, increased weight, tired - inability to manage stress.

Skin effects of stress (76/4)

Skin rashes, hives, eczema, acne, psoriasis, herpes, hair loss, itching.

Respiratory effects of stress (126/18/36)

Tension in the throat and chest may restrict airflow, chest pain/tightness, more than one cold or flu a year, allergies, asthma, chronic bronchitis, choking, dizziness, fainting.

After the 1984 Moscow Olympics, my attention was drawn to a report that all Russian athletes were given the herbal tea *eleutherococcus* (65/2), because it reduces *the level of stress*

(66/3), or *energy surges* (66/3), back to as near normal as possible and quicker than anything else.

There are six letters in the word *stress* (19/1), and we know that every time number 6 appears our attention is directed to the kidneys. Indeed it is reasonable to anticipate that when surges occur, *energy breaks* (60/6) can be expected. The vibration for the herb used is given above and is the same for *stress reduction* (65/2).

Coping with stress (80/8) is the same vibration as for universal energy, as well as for what I term as *relight God's flame* (80/8). This divination is referring to *the attuning of the Divine within the living tissues of the body to the creative energies* (379/19).

As always one can find the negative side of every vibration which, in this instance, reads, *an absence of energy within the body* (154/19), i.e. to *the stress condition* (83/2).

Something on Cancer

Cancer can be called a *catastrophe of form* (83/2). A natural catastrophe leaves chaos in its wake, that is to say an extreme degree of disorganization. This is the real situation in cancer. *When the organizing forces of the ego and the astral body withdraw to a greater or lesser extent, the metabolic organ affected is exposed to external influences and becomes the plaything of chaotic forces* (813/84/93).

Instead of order maintained by the higher constitutional elements (the consciousness), one sees the inner disorder which occurs so frequently in the modern world (673/43/61). The cells, instead of working together in an orderly manner, begin to live a life of their own, to proliferate freely, and to fall prey to influences arising from the physical world.

Forms of attack on the senses, particularly from noise, favour the creation of the state of chaos which one finds in cancer. *Psychic shocks, for example from divorce, also have a trigger effect that can set-off cancer* (833/23/86).

Normal growth is a process of multiplication which is controlled by sculpturing forces. This occurs as a result of two activities, one of multiplication arising from the etheric forces, and the other of *form-building, the sculpturing activity of the forces of the astral body and the ego which transform the etheric forces into formative forces* (598/58).

The tumour itself is really only a sign that the cancer illness has become localized (32/33/42).

The yellow colouring matter in butter is capable of giving rise to cancer of the liver. Thus certain substances have a selective action on certain organs.

It is known that cancer attacks a weak point in the organism for example an organ which has been submitted to a surgical operation more or less recently, or the site of some previous trauma (711/72/81). The idea that a blow on the breast can be a factor giving rise to cancer is a classic example.

The fatigue of a cancer patient is rather more a lack of animation or initiative (320/50).

Some kind of lassitude in cancer patients is noticeable in their expressions. Their eyes appear slightly veiled and their gaze seems to be turned inwards. They give the impression of listening internally (839/29).

One can say that insomnia beginning without evident cause must make one suspect latent cancer (365/32/95). Cancer is much more frequent in women who have been divorced than in married women. One presumes that this results from the extreme psychic stress suffered in divorce.

The visualization of the etheric is very important in making any prognosis for cancer (381/21/39).

The lack of previous illness in cancer patients is striking (233/26/53). They often declare that they have never been ill.

This is partly due to the fact that they have suffered little from febrile conditions owing to their low susceptibility to inflammatory conditions.

Using mistletoe herbal tea concentrates the action around the tumour where it causes hyperaemia and a rise in temperature (467/17/44). This reaction makes it necessary for a certain caution to be exercised in the treatment of cerebral tumours because of the increased intercranial pressure the use of mistletoe might possibly provoke.

Mistletoe appears to repulse the terrestrial forces by behaving in a manner which is opposite of the tumour which opens itself to them. It resists the action of the etheric forces, i.e. proliferative forces (843/33/87).

The aim of any treatment of cancer must be to renew the equilibrium between the structural forces and the forces of proliferation (528/51/78). Firstly, there is the reinforcement of the organism's defences and form-giving powers. Secondly, a furtherance of the metamorphosis of the vegetative (etheric) forces must be achieved. *Cancer prevention includes the need to work on the process of metamorphosis of the etheric forces into thought forces* (502/52). This should be carried out at the time when this normally occurs, i.e. during the school years.

[Note: The advantages of the Reiki technique are discussed elsewhere. Suffice to say here that, in learning Reiki, one is taught how to *balance the chakras as well as the aura* (109/19), along with *accessing healing energy through the feet* (189/99)].

Bowel Cancer (47/2)

I have always maintained that bowel cancer goes hand-in-hand with deficient thyroid activity. Several divinations are particularly relevant:

- *deficient thyroid energy may cause bowel cancer*

(207/27).
- *a thyroid energy deficiency may lead to bowel cancer* (223/43).
- *a thyroid energy deficiency will reduce the metabolic rate and may cause bowel cancer* (344/74/38).
- *a deficient thyroid energy level will result when there is a tendency to shyness* (343/37/73).

With respect to the last of the divinations, I think it relevant that in vibration 73 one also finds the *retention of waste within the body* (163/73). Taking this one step further, also under this vibration one finds *lymphatic slowness*, which is surely logical.

Then also under vibration 73 one finds *the number of love*, as well as *the brain print* on which I will comment shortly. In the meantime let's quickly refer to vibration 18 where we find *deficient thyroid energy, and any reluctance or unwillingness to love the self will result in deficient thyroid energy* (378/18).

Now what about *the brain print*? It is my absolute conviction that the Reiki technique is the way to alter the brain print, thereby getting the brain to send out different messages. Indeed I am mindful of one man who had had his thyroid removed, whom I trained to Reiki I. Testing beforehand showed a nil energy level, but afterwards there was massive energy at his throat chakra where the thyroid is situated. What was most staggering was the difference in his voice, which sounded quite splendid.

Wholistic interpretation of a body condition or organ can provide some light on problems and their solution:
- *The thyroid: humiliation. I never get what I want to do - when is it going to be my turn?* (353/38/83)
- *Bowel problems: a fear of letting go of the old and no longer needed* (262/82).

You should refer to number 38 mentioned above. Finally, it

is no coincidence that number 82, which I have just mentioned, is the vibration for both *cell regeneration* and *the thyroid gland.*

Multiple Sclerosis (74/2)

For a number of reasons, not the least of which is that the vibration for Bowel Cancer is number 47, I have been intensely interested in Multiple Sclerosis which is under vibration number 74. As always, there are interesting divinations which I hope and believe will add to an understanding of the problem:

- *You may well have a good reason to be angry, but do not allow that anger to get hold of your body* (344/74).
- *Blockages in the throat chakra are a resistance to the feeling of emotion. Always have faith in what you are doing* (434/74/47).
- *Thoughts and feelings are forms that go out and become attached to wherever they may be sent* (344/74).

Under number 74 one finds *masculine energy* - fair enough, because we all have both masculine and feminine energy within. However, as there are clearly more cases of MS in women than men, there appears to be the parameter for conflict, because this vibration also contains *the woman within* - in other words, female energy. Thus the scenario is set, at least in the marriage or partnership context, where *balancing within* (74/2) is needed before those thoughts and feelings go out as forms and become attached to wherever they may be sent, which is presumably to the partner. For, once those thoughts and feelings which necessarily must arise from the balancing within, or the lack thereof, have gone out, who knows in what form they may be returned subsequently? Surely, this scenario explains why one also finds under number 74 *so very insecure, and my burden of fear, as well as my own barriers.*

All I seek to do is to get a new understanding of the MS problem, for I have met or corresponded with some lovely MS sufferers. I have certainly no wish to cause any offence either to any of them or to their respective partners.

Looking a bit further, to try and get some more clues one finds both *fierce emotion,* as well as *an energy volcano,* which is perhaps explainable. Going on one also finds under number 74 *improved brain intercellular activity* (164/74), and how best is this achievable - by using *Reiki Energy* (74/2).

Unlocking all the secret possible health scenarios hidden within these names of ours necessarily takes time. A recent investigation of a client shows that two number 74's come on stream in her life at about age 40 and go through to age 50. She has problems with facial hives. From her age 27 through to her age 40 vibration number (558/54) applies, and reads, *a facial hives rash resulting from an inability to self-express adequately - a sign of frustration and a signal of developing multiple sclerosis* - shades of things to come perhaps, but also a sign of how she currently views her life and even tackles the problem, which depends of course on her willingness to cooperate.

Cholesterol (51/6)

Cholesterol: a clogging of the channels of joy, fear of accepting joy (272/29/92).

My comments:

1. From number 29 we learn:
   - *a pronounced awareness of time, and seemingly dominated by a sense of urgency* (299/29). This comment applies largely to the materialistic or business personality.

- *wanting to win is fine but don't take yourself too seriously* (236/29/56). Again, a reference to the business person.
- *poor protein digestion* (119/29).

This could apply to many, certainly a lot of businessmen.

- *love is the most powerful energy for transmuting* (209/29) - surely this defines the interrelationship with joy, for number 56 asks, *without love how can there be any joy?* It goes on to talk of a liver dysbalance.
- *kidney and liver meridians* (119/29).

Does not this provide the final understanding? I think it does, for *emotions and anger adversely impact on liver function* (222/24/42/6), showing the interrelationship with the kidneys.

2. From number 92 we learn:
- *a selfish materialistic bent is embodied here* (182/11/92). So, here we have another approach to the problem.
- *the shoulders are meant to carry joy, not burdens* (182/92). All I can suggest is that you start looking at others, noticing their bent shoulders (65/2).
- *the physiological state is a macrostate of the same system of which the physical state is a microstate* (362/38/92). So very, very true - what is apparently going on outside is also going on inside.
- *as a living, active individual, you do have certain significant and fundamental controls over your life, and you can make intelligent choices for yourself, and you do have the power within you to restore and maintain your health* (902/92). Yes, so true once again.

3. There seems to a suggestion that cholesterol can be corrected entirely by changing one's diet - maybe, or on the other hand, maybe not. For, by changing one's diet, one hardly changes a physiological state.

4. Reference has been made to *the shoulders* (55) - see above. Now, vibration number 55 covers what I term as *my brain waves*, as well as *the cerebrum*. Thus, the Reiki technique is a very good way to alter the brain's waves. It happens also that it always provides great relief to the many who come for a treatment with *painful shoulders* (74/2).

Last, and by no means least, number 55's depth of wisdom includes, *change occurs only when we are ready for it. We have a choice to consciously create change or wait for circumstances* (perhaps a real health problem) *to create it in us* (525/55/73).

The Belly (37/1)

The belly is the feeling centre of the body-mind (201/21). It is within our bellies that many of our emotions and passions originate.   (500/50/5)

Emotions can be thought of as energy in motion (e-motion) (227/29/47). Once they are created they will attempt to release themselves unless restricted by conflicting body-mind beliefs and mechanisms.   (713/74/83)

From the belly emotions flow downward, surging through the pelvis and legs, flushing the body-mind with sexual energy and power, while serving to ground the torso to the earth through the energetic channels of the legs.   (919/19/91)

[Note: this is what should happen. However, too often, the energy becomes impeded at the pelvis and no grounding takes place].

Other emotions flow upward from the belly through the diaphragm and into the chest. *The chest should amplify the emotions with love and self-assertion* (278/26/98). Depending on what sort of emotions are in play, they may then proceed to the throat, the arms, the mouth, the eyes, etc.   (1077/15/6)

The throat is an avenue of expression, a channel of creativity (244/28/64). Any problems represent an inability to speak up for one's self, swallowed anger, and stifled creativity. There is a refusal to change.   (744/24/78)

Skin problems represent anxiety and fear. There is a feeling of being threatened (336/39/66).

Each body-mind part can be a place where the natural flow of emotions can be restricted or blocked, causing it to become stuck or twisted, and increasingly congested. *Emotional blocks and unexpressed feelings* (160/70) obstruct the flow of emotive energy that streams through the body-mind on its way from creation to expression.   (1212/33)

All feelings, once initiated, must proceed through the four phases of tension, charge, discharge, and relaxation if there is to be a continual purging and self-cleansing of the emotional body-mind. When one or more of the phases is incomplete, *the emotional charge will congest and become energetic debris that accumulates at the point of blockage* (383/23/32), a point which in many instances is the belly. This accumulated debris is first experienced as stress and later as armour, and detracts from the body-mind's natural functioning in a way that encourages conditions of conflict.   (2162/38)

We tend to fool ourselves into believing that if we order an emotion to cease with our intellect, it will disappear without trace from the body-mind. This is not so, for *when an emotion is blocked before it is fully expressed, the energetic charge of the emotion, and of the experience that gave birth to the emotion, becomes stressfully trapped* (704/74) within the part of the body-mind that corresponds to the blockage. In many instances, this part is the gut.   (1771/88/16/7)

The body-mind region tends to shape and form itself around

any *chronically held imploding energy* (173/11/83) and the stressful attitudes that motivate *the energetic blockage* (94/4). This blockage and armour further hamper *the natural flow of life consciousness* (143/17/53) through the congested region. Eventually there will be a breakdown of the body's natural regenerative and rehabilitative processes. (1459/55)

The growth of any idea (emotion) into temporal realization is the result of creative aggression. It is impossible to try to erase true aggression. To do so would be to obliterate life as we know it. (775/55/73)

You cannot restrain energy (119/29), as you may think you can. You simply collect it, whereupon it grows, seeking its fulfilment. (508/58)

The problem is not how to deal with normal aggression, but how to handle it when it has remained unexpressed, ignored and denied over a long period of time. (640/10)

The Tight Neck (58/4) represents conflict between mind and body and over control by the intellect. All too often it displays *difficulty with self-expression and assertion* (196/16).

(642/12/66)

One of the most pertinet divination with respect to *the belly* (37/1) reads appropriately, *"the eye at the centre of a hurricane is a centre of peace, but fraught with power"* (388/37). What this is saying is that *when the emotions are calm, there will be peace within the belly, and when they are not, there will be dark and dangerous energy within* (538/52/88).

This is why one finds Vibration number 88 listing t*he seat of many illnesses* as will as *the act of grounding. It is a fact of life that no one can be "properly grounded" when there is unfolding energy within the belly*(515/56/65).

Next we find more wisdom in Vibration number 56 in the divination which reads, *when you can understand that your lifestyle was a big part in how your disease got going, how the*

167

illness came about, then what life is saying in that a big part of the difficulty is how you deal with stress (776/56/74).

I deal with *"grounding"* (55) at length in my book "The Challenge to teach Reiki" to which I refer you for *Reiki is a wonderful way to move any dark potentially dark and dangerous stagnant energy that is within* (390/30). Finally, it is no accident to find that *the solar plexus energy level* (130/30) in the same vibration.

To Conclude

First let me say "thank you" to you, the reader, for your interest and diligence in remaining with me throughout this gnothological thesis, which I believe will prove to have initiated a completely new and potentially exciting way of looking at personal health and attitudes.

I have thoroughly enjoyed every minute of my researching and, equally so, the writing. Indeed I have personally learnt alot whilst writing, so much so that the book really is the start of what will turn out to be a series of on-going publications on the results of investigating these numbers, these energies within.

The divinations with respect to health have stood and will continue to stand the test of time. So, it is perfectly possible to know at any given period in someone's life, just what body organs are likely to be under maximum usage. The kabala provides this information. After all, the Chinese have known for thousands of years just how the biological clock works, showing exactly which body organs are working at any given time of day.

Remember that just because a certain vibration gives us *Parkinson's disease* (72), this is not in itself *a prediction* (60), it is a guide. Besides appearing in the kabala, such detail can come from the name - for example, if the Christian name Craig (39197) was attached to the surname Barton (213265), where the interlocking letters are G-B = 7-2/72.

This line of thinking does not in itself produce a prediction but is only *a guide* (29). However, if another two number 72's were to be found in the kabala, the prediction would then become confirmed. As it happens they are not in the particular kabala. However, there are three number 79's in the kabala - so what does this mean? Answer - either *bowel elimination*, or *arteriosclerosis*, or *prostate gland cancer*.

It should go without saying that information of this sort is delicate and requires appropriate handling by the professional healer. However perhaps more importantly the message comes out loud and clear ... do not just join any given christian name onto the surname and hope for the best. Maybe you chose a name for your child out of love or maybe just because you liked the name. That is not really the point, for now there is available information about every possible christian name that may be attached to a particular surname to indicate likely health scenarios for the life.

Just about all who consult with me have in my experience *an energy blockage* (75/3). It is so easy to demonstrate this to any client, and usually it is equally easy to know where the blockage is. Perhaps you will appreciate why I have such faith in the Reiki technique. The only rider to add is that for *health improvement* (87) the healer's hands must work from the feet upwards and not head downwards, for *earth energy is healing energy* (153/18/63) - and number 63 is the vibration for *feeling good* and last, but by no means least, *great vitality*.

I am convinced that *Reiki energy* (74/2) may very well contain the answer to *multiple sclerosis* (74/2). Within this vibration one finds *stifled emotions* (74/2), which is what I believe MS to really be all about. As a Reiki Master teacher I am privileged to observe the changes that occur in students. It is wonderful to see. Reiki is so gentle, so good at releasing *the muscle reflexes* (74/2), and thereby *the tenseness resulting from stifled or blocked emotions* (222/24/42). I suggest that it could even prove to be *the miracle cure* (69/6), at least for some sufferers.

It so happens the vibration number 83 contains the definition of both the wholistic understanding of multiple sclerosis and the thyroid. (see defs...) So much of my work shows that the people who have these stifled emotions are those who have *a self-expression holding-back* (120/30). Invariably, associated with this is *imbalanced energy in the thyroid gland* (174/12/84). The Reiki technique can correct all this so easily.

I do not, and will never, apologise to doctors who turn and say, "tests show the thyroid to be normal". Maybe by the medical tests it comes out as *normal* (28/1), and I can accept this. However, the medical tests do not contain any relative measurement of *the thyroid gland* (82/1) and *the solar plexus energy level* (120/30). This is where the imbalance occurs.

You must tie this all together and draw your own conclusions. I believe, and am certain, that the answers are all there, both for MS and many other problems. To put it quite simply, if I can regain the ability to use my own eyes for reading, without reading spectacles, after all the tales of gloom that the optician gave me - "you know, at age 42 you are getting on, you must expect your eyes to go backwards" - incredible but true, believe me, if I can do it, so too can you.

The choice of a name for a child should be treated responsibly (243/27/63). It is not and never will be "a lucky dip", nor should it ever be a question of a particular name suddenly becoming in vogue. As I write I understand that the name *Rhiannon* (49/4) is now in vogue. I cannot think of a harder name to handle. Of course, all or everything is possible, but with a Karma number 16, I wouldn't like to be responsible for labelling a child with that name. But, enough on this, for my forthcoming book on christian or given names will provide plenty of details.

However, I must add that I will personally not have

anything to do with the use of so called nicknames. Quite simply, if a name in itself could only seem to shine if treated as nickname, it is hardly worthy of choice in the first place. All I will add now is - how many fellows can effectively handle the name *Robert* (33), with Karma 23? The answer has to be very few indeed - they all become *Bob* (10), with Karma number 37, which automatically writes *anxiety* (37), *struggle* (37), and *tragedy* (37) into the life, along with potentially unfortunate health such as *a heart attack* (37), *aneurism* (37), or *hernia* (37).

I am sure that my methodology can be successfully used in assessing the work skill potential for individuals, e.g. take the surname Rosenthal (96552813=39) where the overriding letters R-1 = 93, where we find divinations that read, *distinctive energy* (93/3), *a compelling energy* (93/3), and *the creative potential* (93/3). Surely all the attributes for a successful salesman, particularly as the expression number 39/3 reads *enthusiasm.* And what do we find - we find *salesman's skill* (39/3), as well as *sales skills* (30/3). One way or the other, it all does tie in.

Now have a look at the name Mozart (468192) where the overriding letters are M-t = 42. Look also at the name Beethoven (255286455 = 42), and what do we find but *musical skill* (42) - coincidental maybe, but on the other hand maybe not, and certainly there is a great deal of potential research into names that could well produce results which might well prove to be of interest.

I can't believe it to be coincidental that under vibration number 81 one finds several divinations that explain *breast cancer* (46/1): *resentment piled-up* (81/9), *the lack of self-worth* (81/9), *needing validity* (81/9), *dangerous energy* (81/9), *a poor metabolic rate* (81/9), and *breast cancer developing* (81/9). The answers surely lie both in the sympathetic numerological interpretation of the energies within the name, along with a balancing of the client's chakras, probably using Reiki.

I am quite delighted with *the twists and turns along my path* (118/19/28) that have confronted my life. Sure, *my early scepticism* (84/3) has dissolved and I have *come back to God* (51/6). I hope you can align with *the God concept* (63/9). *God* (17/8) occurs in every number vibration in one form of words or another, for *diversity* (52/7) is really what God is all about.

Recapturing Health (87/6)

Most people silently suffer in stagnated lives (177/87/6). Good health and prosperity does occur in life but do you have such a life? Will you ever? Will your one special time, your only time in all eternity, pass without you ever knowing *good health, prosperity, and real love* (70/7)?

Do you feel energetic and emotionally fulfilled (200/20) - all *energy* (90/9); it is *the light-bringing, or healing energy* (190/10/1). The Reiki technique (97/7) is a very useful tool in making this *spiritual energy* (84/3) available to *the world* (42/6). Let us all be so grateful to *the Universe* (56/2) for enabling Dr Mikao Usui to find *the hidden symbols* (76/4) originally used by Buddha for healing.

A surprising number of people can actually see with their eyes what is sometimes called *orgone energy* (78/6), and yet, incredibly, they cannot or do not know how to "access that energy". *The Master symbol* (62/8) Dia ko mio, that the Reiki Master uses, is the same vibration as *the Hand of God* (62/8), *the invisible* (62/8), and *a model of health* (62/8).

This is no coincidence: it is totally logical: it is the reason why you should, indeed you must, investigate further.

The Hidden Wisdom within Numbers

The Key to Life Enrichment

You have ventured with me along *the path of knowledge* (87) towards *the horizon* (66). Now the challenge for you and for me is to investigate further the potential that *gnothological understanding* (126/36) of numbers provides to extract and thus reveal *the hidden wisdom within numbers* (146/56), thereby enriching our lives.

So "Harken Ye" to the definition that reads:

The path of knowledge: the path is not endless, is not without its goal (306/36) - and in so doing , note the alignment of vibration number 36.

A. J. Mackenzie Clay,
The Reiki Teaching Centre,
Bungendore,
NSW 2621
Australia

Appendix A - Numbers

The Body Image (62)

- The head (33/6)
- The eyes (33/6)
- The nose (32/5)
- The brain (41/4)
- The neck (30/3)
- The throat (42/6)
- The nails (34/7)
- The chest (34/7)
- The breath (42/6)
- The heart (40/4)
- The skin (32/5)
- The digestion (63/9)
- The metabolic rate (67/4)
- The intestines (59/6)
- The immune system (67/4)
- Lymph activation (73/1)
- The nerves (44/8)
- The waist line (55/1)
- The legs (31/4)
- The feet (33/6)
- The subconscious brain (84/3)
- The instinctive mind of the solar plexus (163/1)
- The solar plexus (60/6)
- The abdominal brain (76/4)
- The seat of the emotions (89/8)
- The still small voice from within (135/9)
- The voice of higher reason (127/1)
- The Sympathetic Nervous System (121/4)
- The gastrointestinal tract (100/1)
- Peristaltic action (81/9)
- The feeling brain (81/9)
- The sense organs (67/4)
- The gut feelings (67/4)
- God's own plexus (59/5)
- The body (36/9)
- The hair (42/6)
- The ears (31/4)
- The mouth (38/2)
- The shoulders (55/1)
- The arms (30/3)
- The hands (34/7)
- The lungs (34/7)
- The respiration (78/6)
- The kidneys (48/6)
- The adrenals (44/8)
- The liver (45/9)
- The bowels (37/1)
- The bladder (43/7)
- The stomach (40/4)
- The muscles (34/7)
- The circulation (68/5)
- The hips (40/4)
- The knees (33/6)

- The gonads (39/3)
- The toes (29/2)
- The conscious brain (78/6)
- The emotional nature of man (103/4)
- The great plexus (64/1)
- The thinking brain (88/7)
- The Cerebrospinal Nervous System (135/9)
- The mind (37/1)

10

- The state of supraconsciousness (100/10).
- If you have faith as tiny as a mustard seed, nothing shall be impossible to you (280/10).
- Sei he ki, the symbolic key to accessing mental energy (640/10).

11

- Guilt is the teacher, love is the lesson (146/11).
- A closed heart will kill you (101/11).
- The path to a higher consciousness (137/11).
- No man ever becomes great or good except through many and great mistakes (281/11/29)

12

- Behind thought stands the whole force of nature (192/12)
- The wholistic approach to health (138/12).
- Controlling the secret forces of nature (165/12).

13

- Begin to change by softening the mould (157/13).
- The realm of the mind is universal (121/13).
- The physical body is but a reflection of the subtle energies within, which are themselves a reflection of the cosmos (463/13).

14

- Spiritual fire energy (113/14).
- Symbols are to the mind what tools are to the hand. Knowledge of the highest forms of existence is obtained by a process other than thought (194/14).

- The overself, the aura, the unseen (122/14).

15

- The world is your mirror (123/15).
- The teapot can be likened to the mind (132/15).
- Guilt is the bitter pill that was injected into society, by society. It keeps you in the status quo of lack of self-empowerment (465/15).

16

- The universe is God's energy (124/16).
- Nature is intelligent because it is too complicated to be called anything else (286/16).
- The invisible organizing principles of nature, rather being eternally fixed, evolve along with the systems they organize (556/16).

17

- Love is where there is faith (125/17).

- Tension: a sign of an energy blockage (143/17).
- If you can't give, you can't receive (134/17).

18

- A mind in a state of miracle readiness (135/18).
- "Not thinking" as one knows it (108/18).
- If you know you are wise, find the "key" (153/18).

19

- The vibration of universal energy (145/19).
- The body is that part of the soul that shows (154/19).
- The rise and fall of the cosmic tides (136/19).

20

- "Light": that seemingly illusive force that is always available even in the dark (290/20).
- Anyone who has succeeded in developing an awareness will get progressively drawn onto and along the path to the light (470/20).

- The power of the symbol to influence consciousness (200/20).

21

- A need for "grounding" to something bigger than oneself (237/21).
- One's feet represent one's understanding of oneself, of life, of others (291/21).
- You achieve a sense of balancing by becoming "at one with nature" (237/21).

22

- Touching the Source is how the mind creates its patterns of intelligence (292/22).
- The common characteristic of love between equals is a desire for mutual help (292/22).
- God, love, and life are one and the same. They are the truth (211/22).

23

- In the radiance of love and wisdom, one learns the secrets of the universe (284/23).
- The triumph of imagination over intelligence (212/23).
- As you are an aware soul, "a guide" will help you on the path to the Light (257/23).

24

- All of man's earthly problems are created by his thought projections (267/24).
- What we see is governed largely by what we expect to see (213/24).
- Total upheaval in your life brings new opportunities (231/24).

25

- It is the love of money which is the root of all evil (214/25).
- The root cause of cancer may well be a lack of greenness in the life (241/25).
- The tongue is recognised as the opening to the heart (223/25).

26

- One's signature reveals the energy that is currently available (242/26).
- Effective change requires commitment, agreement, surrender, and action (296/26).
- Stop, look, listen: one remembers what one wants to remember (215/26).

27

- Being obstinate imprisons a man in his own sin and darkness (207/27).
- Awakening is a process that has many levels. It goes on unfolding in its own time (297/27).
- Take charge of your own destiny as a basis for shaping the future (234/27).

28

- Flashes of direct intuition - the future as based on probabilities (273/28).
- Every man individualizes the Infinite through his speech (211/28).
- A spiritual being tries to become human and not the other way around (262/28).

29

- I have a very special need for lots of tender loving care right now (281/29).
- Spiritual growth is our only purpose and reason for being alive on earth. Every person must learn how to utilise energy for spiritual growth and constructive purposes. Positive use of energy raises the level of consciousness, or it raises a person's vibrational rate or frequency (1163/29).
- Be convinced, for there is incalculable power at your fingertips (272/29).

30

- The pathway to the Horizon (120/30).
- The Cosmos, the source of all energy is accessible only through full mind usage (300/30).
- The Universe will provide

(330/30).

- The health of your self-image (120/30).

31

- Only a new sense of direction will get you out of trouble and enable you to leave the past behind (355/31).
- The goal should be to create a body/personality that can fully express the divine creative spirit, a form that can do everything the spirit within wants to do easily, skilfully and beautifully (751/31).
- The long awaited sunrise occurs (121/31).

32

- Many of the secrets of life lie hidden in the mystical formulae of numerical divination (365/32).
- It is not uncommon to find a resistance to the nature and energy of a number missing from the name (374/32).
- Wouldn't life be so dull without some problems of some sort (212/32)?

33

- Perfection is not static, it is dynamic. Not "I am what I am" but "I am what I am becoming" (303/33).
- He who is aware of his own true self, the Divinity within him, can do the so-called impossible (375/33).
- Number 3 stands for "self-arousal" and number 33 therefore calls for "real life action" (303/33).

34

- Life does not discriminate against us. We discriminate against ourselves by the poor orders we give our subconscious minds (484/34).
- The moment you set a goal, you identify the problems involved in obtaining the goal, but these are soluble (394/34).
- Any revelation of a deeper reality carries enormous

power with it - one taste alone can make life undeniably worthwhile (484/34).

35

- To fully appreciate light, it is necessary to first experience and understand darkness (341/35).
- Life is being able to move out to others and this can't be done fully until there is an acceptance of oneself (386/35).
- Presence has to do with your spirit body being in the same time frame as your physical body (377/35).

36

- Most people are asleep and not even paying attention to what is going on around them (324/36).
- It is "the now" that is important, providing as it does an opportunity to change the detrimental aspects in one's personality and character so that the future will be enhanced

(666/36).
- My fear of letting go of the old and no longer needed (216/36).

37

- Prudence means skill in right thinking and in the performance of right action (343/37).
- Fortitude means constant courage, patience, and endurance without fear of danger (307/37).
- "Duality" indicates a balanced partnership in which neither parts dominates, each having his or her own space and vibrations, but blending together in one complementary whole (847/37).

38

- The happiest man is he whose pleasures are cheapest (218/38).
- Will a problem or ill-health disappear soon? If it doesn't, you will have set it up "not to happen" (362/38).

- Sometimes an individual has to go to the very bottom before he asks for help and starts again on the way up (398/38).

39

- Success comes from learning to choose the right time for the right action (309/39).
- The sign of accumulated tension is when one stands with one's feet in different directions (318/39).
- Do not be too desperate for a relationship or you are likely to be disappointed or not find a satisfactory one. So do not become too emotionally attached to the desire. Often it is better to have your attention elsewhere (849/39).

40

- The beneficial energy that creates and drives the cosmos (220/40).
- The model of health or of illness (130/40).
- The feeling of being

grounded in someone else's shoes (220/40).

41

- The ego is related to an increased probability of heart attacks and premature death. One test is how many times a person says "I", "me", "mine" (491/41).
- Irrational "should statements" rest on the assumption that you are entitled to instant gratification at all times (401/41).
- A life that is out of balance may call for a sacrifice of some sort to bring about a better appreciation of relative values (437/41).

42

- The power of the mind by which it immediately perceives the truth of things without reasoning or analysis (465/42).
- Do not demand that the order of things occur in any exact way, for then there is no flexibility. Let

go of expectation (411/42).

- Men in the materialistic world are trying to get for themselves all possible for some future day which may never come (465/42).

43

- The tongue is recognized as the opening to the heart (223/43).
- The tendency of man is to belittle himself by constantly rating himself in comparison with how others appear to him (475/43).
- Life does not discriminate against us. We discriminate against ourselves by the poor orders we give our subconscious minds (484/43).

44

- It is so important to preserve the process of imagination and to reach ut beyond the concrete und physical (431/44).
- Experience is the name everyone gives to his

mistakes (224/44).

- Regret and remorse both imply a holding on to the past (224/44).

45

- Your moods and actions should be seen as a result of rewards and punishment from your environment. If you are feeling depressed and doing nothing about it, it follows that your behaviour is being rewarded in some way (855/45).
- It is a tragedy that so many of the youth of the world hasten into marriage, untrained, unfit, and without preparation (468/45).
- Resistance to anything, such as change, is what makes you tired (225/45).

46

- When the thymus gland is closed, or partly so, the heart connection is lessened, and there is much more chance of being

unwell (478/46).
- You can learn from everything (136/46).
- A magnetism that is extremely attractive to the opposite sex (226/46).

47

- There is one and one only person in the world who has the power to threaten your self-esteem, and that is - you (425/47).
- Life is kind really, for it invariably presents another opportunity to make good on past errors (407/47).
- If one believes that abundant good is available to one, one will find abundant good in every area of one's experience (443/47).

48

- The ability to live to a great age without falling prey to disease reflects one's ability to mobilize one's consciousness (462/48).
- A properly grounded person will be fit and well and able to access energy from the earth through the feet (426/48).
- The so-called qualities of health and illness define each other, just as do the north and south poles (417/48).

49

- Fear is what keep us separate from others. Fear is what alienates us from nature. Fear is what causes our estrangement from God (463/49).
- Have you ever felt that it is probably useless to try and know God as a being, a thinking, loveable, conscious and available being? (472/49).
- A person's awareness will be responsible for his own cancer (229/49).

50

- Soul-making occurs when the psyche is wounded and may be likened to the penetration of the ova by the sperm (410/50).

- Let the light from your future self draw you upwards from that rich soil of experience, for it is a rich experience (500/50).
- As the fifth chakra is the chakra of judgement, it is important to try and literally let go of all ill-feelings one may be harbouring towards anyone. When angry one becomes bonded to a person, which serves only to perpetuate the ill-feeling (950/50).

(91/10/1)

- pure consciousness heals
- psychological stresses
- a personal recycling
- the feeling of guilt
- heightened awareness
- the lure of the easy way
- the brain chemistry
- the tyranny of more
- grace under pressure
- the unwellness potential
- health maximization
- dammed-up sexual energy
- the liver meridian
- a body chemical imbalance
- a kidney deficiency

- my emotional prison
- impeded circulation
- highly adrenalised
- the fatigue syndrome
- hypothyroidism

(82/10/1)

cell regeneration
hardness of thought
spiritual healing
my poor self-image
the inner vision
my habitual complexes
nearing the answers
- rekindle the heart
- the ability to relax
- my banked-up energy
- self-organization
- my false brain signals
- the thyroid gland
- kidney discomfort
- a thyroid dysbalance
- chemical toxicity
- a low thymus reading
- leg muscles disorders
- cancer of the lymph
- sleep deprivation

(73/10/1)

- mastering the self
- a dormant kundalini
- pure consciousness
- chronic self-blame

- the survival chakra
- my own barriers
- my inner guide
- a cold personality
- vertical growth
- a loss of sexual drive
- the number of love
- heart connection
- lymphatic slowness
- rheumatic fever
- massive coronary
- a glandular problem
- stomach disorders
- a weight problem
- high uric acid
- a manic depressive

(64/10/1)

- self-revelation
- my limitations
- heaven on earth
- mental confusion
- the strong flame
- my suffering
- a beacon of light
- a state of inertia
- mental imagery
- my aggression
- my confidence
- the restless mind
- The heart chakra
- undetected cancer
- quantum healing

- tenosynovitis
- a full deep breath
- cold, white hands
- toxic residues
- stagnant energy

(55/10/1)

- the way to teach
- my unaware soul
- mental capacity
- my brain waves
- social virtue
- few friends
- self-reliance
- insecurity
- discipline
- absolute disaster
- sound judgement
- failure awaits
- extreme stress
- my glandular system
- a blocked pelvis
- heart ailments
- my saliva glands
- nephritis
- exhausted muscles
- lymph cancer

(92/11/2)

- harmonious resonance
- unexpressed feelings
- highly intuitive
- conflicting desires

- a heightened awareness
- playing with fire
- genuine self-interest
- without a sense of health
- the challenge to change
- an obstructive energy
- the ultimate motivation
- the forest of failure
- thymus underactivity
- intestinal infection
- frequent urination
- kidney functioning
- pancreatic malfunction
- constipation headaches
- emotionally disturbed
- the brain's chemistry

(83/11/2)

- driving ambition
- total unreliability
- good communication
- turbulent emotional sea
- reasoning ability
- stereotyped outlook
- the path to knowledge
- more drive needed
- natural musical ability
- an attitudinal problem
- a very nice person
- blinded by anger
- abdominal disorders
- bronchial problems
- high cholesterol

- cancer of the liver
- prostate infection
- cardiovascular disease
- cold feet in winter
- excessive protein and fat

(74/11/2)

- social confidence
- a tendency to brood
- a sense of wellbeing
- mental strangulation
- physical awareness
- affected by others
- the spirit mind
- fierce emotion
- self-discipline
- given to failure
- untapped potential
- fearful of change
- painful shoulders
- the muscles and nerves
- multiple sclerosis
- cancer of the bowel
- compulsive eating
- weight increase
- menopause problems
- allergy problem

(65/11/2)

- a sense of mission
- a repressed ego
- self-development
- confrontation

- a remarkable stamina
- quite reactive
- very creative
- so unpredictable
- the top echelon
- self-righteous
- relaxed alertness
- high tension
- throat problems
- short of breath
- glandular fever
- trembling hands
- excess mineral salts
- bladder problems
- blocked energy
- food allergies

(56/11/2)

- a researcher
- aloof and distant
- a cosmic force
- mental discord
- a discipline
- no lifeline
- involvement
- a lack of control
- natural audacity
- jog yourself
- liver disease
- small intestines
- peptic ulcer
- constipation
- chest problems

- my lazy bowels
- an ovarian cyst
- a squeaky voice

(93/12/3)

- the pulsating energy
- the whip of my guilt
- vibrational harmony
- my stored up resentment
- the gift of knowledge
- motivational paralysis
- the God within me
- a self-destructive plunge
- a spirit of goodwill
- unintegrated idealism
- the journey forward
- a totally negative attitude
- a constipation problem
- a brainwave abnormality
- high blood pressure
- sexual pressure and guilt
- the kidney meridian
- sexually disconnected
- emotional instability
- iatrogenic problems

(84/12/3)

- miracles of the mind
- a taker, not a giver, I be
- individual awareness
- total trauma in my life
- if I want to, I can do it
- a very fraught time

- the soul or character
- self-gratification
- the art of serenity
- an attitudinal conflict
- respect for others
- pompous and arrogant
- lymph circulation
- loss of muscular control
- a zinc deficiency
- thyroid problems
- weariness and fatigue
- glandular disorders
- kidney filtration
- poor bowel movement

(75/12/3)

- Inner harmony
- twisted thinking
- I am pure spirit
- my hidden anger
- personal magnetism
- emotional anguish
- a strong sexual nature
- sexual indecision
- accessing energy
- overconfidence
- self-understanding
- self-gratification
- excessive weight
- poor bowel action
- the nape of the neck
- an energy blockage
- shallow breathing

- my potbelly stomach
- a heart condition
- the loss of taste and smell

(66/12/3)

- The overcomer
- my frustration
- a state of knowledge
- personal darkness
- my creativity
- energy surges
- my innovations
- total dishonesty
- true thinking
- random thoughts
- self-confidence
- excessive anger
- waste filtration
- rheumatic pain
- the pituitary
- liver problems
- the blood supply
- an exhausted heart
- muscular activity
- nervous tension

(57/12/3)

- a man of vision
- argumentative
- a sense of health
- unambitiousness
- my happiness
- my worries

- serving God
- is there a God?
- quick to mature
- running away
- moral courage
- lost dignity
- excess weight
- cardiac arrest
- abdominal pain
- foot problems
- confined toes
- lymphadenoma
- my hormones
- breast problems

(94/13/4)

- my spiritual growth
- my inner disorders
- the event called knowing
- the all illusive harmony
- the Godliness within
- emotional distortion
- personal maximisation
- an energy explosion
- the human imagination
- inadequacy and failure
- many new experiences
- breathtaking antagonism
- declining eyesight
- clotting abnormalities
- deficient chromium
- the existence of cancer
- lymphatic disorders

- circulatory problems
- enzymatic digestion
- a depressed immune system

(85/13/5)

- the conscious awareness
- preconceived ideas
- understanding nature
- self-induced conflict
- my energy to share
- my unresolved anger
- unfolding meaning
- I am what I am, so selfish
- correct thinking
- self-induced conflict
- my point of mastery
- my midlife crisis
- the metabolism of sugar
- cancer of the pancreas
- repressed sexuality
- lacking any energy
- degenerative joints
- breathing problems
- anxiety disorders
- suicidal depression

(76/13/4)

- magnetic energy
- internal conflicts
- a spiritual pathway
- the karmic reward
- the higher self

- hateworthy actions
- a mind with light
- the fear of illness
- discrimination
- critical and trite
- genuine self-esteem
- anxiety neurosis
- bowel inflammation
- urinary troubles
- chronic fatigue
- poor digestion
- irregular sleep
- shakiness in the arm
- the kidney organs
- a cancerous growth

(67/13/4)

- so very gifted
- so frightened
- the stream of love
- the untouched soul
- the life force
- so very selfish
- really living
- feeling so unsafe
- a keen sense of balance
- overindulgent
- character itself
- avid disbelief
- liver problems
- constipated bowels
- tenosynovitis
- my thigh muscles

- epileptic fit
- a damaged brain cell
- the lymph nodes
- exhausted pancreas

(58/13/4)

- in the Light
- discontentment
- great vision
- guilt complex
- imagination
- emotional blocks
- the subconscious
- anger and fear
- untold riches
- a tragedy looms
- real feeling
- still energy
- dizzy spells
- a blood problem
- gastric cancer
- salivary glands
- bowel problems
- clogged colon
- weight gain
- kidney disease

(95/14/5)

- living in the Light
- the dormant consciousness
- the creativity factor
- a punishment conscience
- life's opportunities

- travelling - but, where to?
- the quality of desire
- my wishful thinking
- early obstacles but later success
- lack of personal self-esteem
- self-initiated effort
- moral self-justification
- a high blood sugar level
- fatigue and depression
- a thyroid disorder
- distorted brain signals
- intestinal dysfunction
- fatigue and depression
- the neuro-transmitters
- atrophy of the brain

(86/15/5)

- an irresistible magic
- rekindle thy heart
- a deepening awareness
- a life balancing signal
- the right timing
- the wrong goal line
- a personal power spot
- self-limiting habits
- silent intelligence
- a dramatic awakening
- very good judgement
- how stupid can you get?
- a disease of the pancreas
- the pituitary gland
- heart fibrillation

- severe cardiac arrest
- serious depression
- electronic warfare
- motor neuron disease
- psychosomatic disease

(77/14/5)

- the spiritual path
- so much happiness
- problems are messages
- drained energy
- lofty aspirationspushing against it
- a high achiever
- the human armoury
- personal equality
- an element of greed
- my love for nature
- going nowhere
- shortness of breath
- nervous mannerisms
- diabetes insipidus
- iron absorption
- chronic obesity
- viral infections
- ulcerative colitis
- allergy responses

(68/14/5)

- the dance of life
- a mind in the dark
- a caring person
- patronizing

- the universal soul
- pain and despair
- inventive ideas
- fear creates evil
- miracles happen
- very depressed
- a joy to live with
- find contentment
- the bowel process
- kidney failure
- lymphatic system
- lead poisoning
- intestinal disease
- skin afflictions
- clots in the veins
- no sexual interest

(59/14/5)

- the master mind
- thinking small
- illumination
- anger prone
- my excitement
- trepidation
- strong willed
- a fragile ego
- self-imagery
- disenchantment
- social service
- controversy
- diabetes mellitus
- the intestines
- kidney disease

- the vagus nerve
- a low body store
- osteoporosis
- high aluminium
- acute pyelitis

(96/15/6)

- the power of the mind
- mirrors of the mind
- the challenge of change
- a heart that has become dry
- beyond new frontiers
- marriage tribulation
- an empathy for people
- an impersonal energy
- to climb every mountain
- no personal motivation
- reaching out for God
- my unhappy body-mind
- a copper deficiency
- an irregular heartbeat
- coronary thrombosis
- a lack of silicon reserve
- nerve and muscle function
- a suppressed immune system
- the sodium/potassium balance
- my chronic bad posture

(87/15/6)

- a man with real vision

- repressed feelings
- a deep sense of meaning
- paralysed thinking
- the point of mastery
- an energy disarray
- my personal growth
- the little selfish ego
- an advanced spiritual status
- an antagonist of nature
- vibrational empathy
- the midlife crisis
- weakness in the kidneys
- high potassium levels
- premenstrual tension
- a diabetes personality
- kidney inflammation
- degenerative disease
- a severe blood problem
- stored fats in the blood

(78/15/6)

- the Golden Flame
- the void of darkness
- the Intuitive Self
- disequilibrium
- the time to celebrate
- expect a severe trauma
- the secret healing
- you must be born again
- accessing excellence
- scared of the future
- an enlarged prostate

- no sexual motivation
- skin irritation
- kidney secretions
- chronically obese
- heart palpitations
- lymph malfunction
- tension in the legs

(69/15/6)

- inspired ideas
- inner turmoil
- emotional poise
- abnormal emotions
- the heart center
- a need to set new goals
- love: the key to joy
- more haste, less speed
- a man with vision
- total lack of control
- openness and appeal
- action not chatter
- kidney problems
- nervous headaches
- rheumatic heart
- blurred vision
- false brain signals
- a blood disorder
- menstrual problems
- a low potassium level

(51/15/6)

- Confidence
- a holding back

- close to nature
- the big ego
- the think-tank
- tribulation
- achievement
- aggression
- curiosity
- drifting
- public acclaim
- very naive
- heart disease
- cholesterol
- kidney stones
- neck problems
- the weight
- a liver trauma
- sexual distress
- very bad asthma

(97/16/7)

- potential maximisation
- self-defeating emotions
- my meaning and purpose
- my self-gratification
- my healing energies
- all my locked-in energy
- the programmed brain
- my self-imposed illnesses
- the number of knowledge
- an obsession for money
- touching infinity
- lacking a morphic balance
- damaged kidney function

- ionising radiation
- blocked lymph drainage
- a toxic blood condition
- severe epileptic fits
- neck and shoulder tension
- high rates of heartbeat
- a coronary thrombosis

(88/16/7)

- my inner knowledge
- incredibly stubborn
- moving with change
- complete frustration
- reaching out to touch
- a self-defeating attitude
- my inner harmony
- a problem from the past
- ebullient confidence
- complete frustration
- harmony and service
- a heavy family burden
- colonic dysfunction
- the onset of adult diabetes
- dangerous toxic levels
- cancerous lymph nodes
- conception problems
- depression and deadness
- tightness in the chest
- a lethargic feeling

(79/16/7)

- those elusive answers
- an inability to bend

- the new consciousness
- the worried look
- play of consciousness
- feeling so guilty
- the symbol for love
- the need to reach out
- social interaction
- so basically insecure
- real business rewards
- greedy for money
- cancer of the rectum
- Alzheimer's disease
- arteriosclerosis
- valvular heart disease
- petit mal epilepsy
- bowel elimination
- the renal arteries
- hormonal problems

(61/7)

- the excitement
- feeling unsafe
- the God forces
- mental disarray
- absolute delight
- suppressed sadness
- concentration
- emotional unease
- accomplishment
- unhappy moods
- health is wealth
- low self-interest
- colonic cancer

- bowel inaction
- sexual discontent
- bad bronchitis
- ovarian cancer
- loss of appetite
- migraine attacks
- toxic products

(52/7)

- the ideal self
- such stubbornness
- nature's secrets
- my stiff neck
- self-motivated
- the struggle
- I am a winner
- unadventurous
- leadership
- disinterest
- mental alertness
- a feared event
- liver damage
- depression
- muscular weakness
- lymph nodes
- wake up tired
- kidney stones
- neck problems
- the pituitary

(98/17/8)

- properly grounded
- emotionally constipated

- the reversal of ageing
- the cancer personality
- a totally positive attitude
- very dangerous energy
- my cosmic electricity
- early childhood trauma
- the builder of the body
- a shrinking signature
- cellular regeneration
- difficult to live with
- pancreatic dysfunction
- psychological disease
- muscular hypertension
- bronchial contraction
- coronary heart disease
- chronic nephritis
- my gastrointestinal tract
- the digestive enzymes

(89/17/8)

- listening to the music
- the road is blocked ahead
- my divine potential
- such a cold personality
- the Ground of Being
- a cloudy stagnated mind
- spiritual progress
- missed opportunity
- One's point of mastery
- no depth of feeling
- my challenge and adventure
- a particularly sad life

- cancer of the cervix
- cervical spondylosis
- hormonal malfunction
- menstruation problems
- the bladder meridian
- a sexual energy blockage
- my poor breathing
- bipolar depression

(71/8)

- upwards and onwards
- the need to change
- real creativity
- hardness of heart
- personal control
- not reaching out
- assertive effort
- emotional blockages
- problem solving
- faulty thinking
- individuality
- a personal torment
- hysterectomy
- haemorrhoids
- the menstrual cycle
- pancreatic cancer
- the hardened neck
- hypertension
- a blood condition
- kidney activity

(62/8)

- the love force

- hidden anger
- the body image
- no confidence
- a mind as clear as a bell
- mental gymnastics
- calm and dependable
- tension and stress
- rational action
- rash decisions
- the cosmic tide
- self-withdrawal
- stomach problems
- foul intestines
- the thymus gland
- heart problems
- the bowel action
- the body fluids
- the thyroid
- the renal veins

(53/8)

- the doorway
- don't miss the bus
- a focussed awareness
- mentally lazy
- light magic
- frustration
- my awakening
- the law of karma
- really alive
- a dead end street
- metaphysical
- blind belief

- lymph system
- wakes up tired
- prostate gland
- sexual decline
- body armour
- my shoulders
- advanced cancer
- brain tumour

(99/18/9)

- my very good judgement
- discordant musical chords
- the search for meaning
- an incoherent meaning
- creative visualization
- the devilish love of self
- accessing quantum healing
- an energy dysfunction
- motivation by curiosity
- poor problem-solving
- life-lifting capacity
- psychological defences
- physical elimination
- coronary heart disease
- my hostility and anger
- imprisoned energy
- hyperthyroidism
- chronic constipation
- imprisoned energy
- so emotionally disturbed

(81/9)

- An inner harmony

- the frustrated bird
- reach out and fear not
- a deep need to feel safe
- spiritual growth
- my unconscious habits
- knowledge and wisdom
- a ferocious temper
- an emerging gift
- a less energised soul
- my hidden powers
- severe depression
- poor circulation
- schizophrenia
- nervous digestion
- pain in the liver
- the thyroid gland
- toxic metal invasion
- hormonal activity
- stones in the pancreas

(72/9)

- absolute brilliance
- self-deprecating
- capacity to change
- a creature of habit
- inner strength
- pent-up resentment
- cockpit potential
- cockpit turbulence
- a strong self-image
- a childhood trauma
- acute perception
- high stress levels

- diverticulitis
- Parkinson's disease
- sluggish kidneys
- gaseous digestion
- poor circulation
- the breath function
- my lymph problems
- weakness in the knees

(63/9)

- the inner self
- my clouded mind
- feeling good
- emotional pain
- so very successful
- my ignorance
- my intuition
- my darkest hour
- a fortunate life
- self-limiting
- a healthy image
- an energy sink
- bronchial asthma
- period pains
- mucous-lined areas
- the digestion
- my arthritis
- cervical cancer
- kidney troubles
- glandular disease

(54/9)

- a visionary

- frustration
- self-assertion
- so very lazy
- born to succeed
- my inactions
- inner peace
- biting sarcasm
- sexual pleasures
- permissive
- so full of ideas
- a silly attitude
- alkaline stomach
- duodenal ulcer
- aorta artery
- a brain tumour
- bronchitis
- throat cancer
- skin problems
- thigh muscles

(46/10)

- self mastery
- the unknown
- the shutters
- the easy way
- a soul crisis
- eternity
- fortitude
- temperance
- excitement
- capability
- diplomacy
- arrogance

- vacillation

(55/10)

- broadminded
- thin-skinned
- down to earth
- real problems
- auric debris
- grounding
- the shoulders
- peak energy
- negative karma
- my gland system
- perfect balance
- the way to teach
- the awakening
- discipline
- wrong habits
- self-reliance
- insecurity
- initiative
- predicaments
- new strengths
- boundless wisdom
- my knowledge
- my whole self
- mental capacity

Glossary A

The Spiritual Life (80/8)

Channel (30/3)

A means of passing or conveying: means of communication: *a one-way path for a signal* (96/6). (340/70)

Channel (your) (55/1)

Balance is an important quality to use in building the structure of your channel. If you have been extreme in one direction you may have to go to the extreme in the other direction inorder to *integrate and balance* (75/3) both aspects of everything (1027/19).

Channel (your) (55/1)

Once you have experienced and released *blocked emotions from the past* (114/15/24), *a greater flow of energy and vitality will enrich your life* (267/24/87). If you are in touch with your feelings as they arise, they can continue to move through and your channel will remain clear (1094/13).

Channelling energy (91/1)

As you become increasingly conscious of *the flow of the universe* (103/13) moving through you and through everything and everyone else, *your body will become capable of channelling more energy (240/60). The more energy you are willing to receive, the more you will be able to give* (325/37/55). (1194/24)

Channelling energy (91/1)

People who have tapped *the universal energy* (95/5) and are willing and prepared to share this energy with others, are the people travelling along *the path to The Light* (85/4), attracting others as they go. These are they who will develop *noticeable auras* (56/2). These are they who are really powerful (1212/33).

Channelling (spontaneous) (93/3)

The more you are willing to surrender *to the energy within you* (109/19), the more power can flow through you (538/52/88).

Enlightenment (65/2)

Enlightenment of the form happens through a miraculous process. As the ego surrenders to *trusting the universe* (94/4), *the spirit penetrates every cell of the body* (188/17/98), *transforming darkness into light* (143/17/53). (868/58/85)

Feeling (40/4)

An intuitive belief (84/3). (124/16/34)

Feeling (40/4)

The sense of touch (66/3). (106/16)

Feeling and desire (83/2)

The intelligent power by which nature and the senses are moved (335/38/65).

Feelings (bottled-up) (75/3)

When we bottle-up our feelings, we close off the life energy flowing through our bodies (375/15/33). The energy of these *unfelt, unexpressed feelings* (116/17/26) remains blocked in our bodies, causing *emotional and physical discomfort* (142/16/52), and eventually *illness and disease* (63/9). (1056/12)

Gratification (postponed) (112/13/22)

There are some very good reasons why we can't have just exactly what we want. Not only can we always have what we want, *we can't always have what we want when we want it* (153/18/63). One of the necessities for travelling the road of your spiritual journeys is to learn to postpone gratification. (1161/27)

Gratitude (42/6)

Gratitude is *thankfulness to those who have helped you* (157/13/67) create your own reality. It is *thankfulness to yourself and your awareness* (158/14/68), to your worth. It is being thankful for the value you are willing to feel. Gratitude is also being thankful that you were willing to create and willing to receive *the love your seen and unseen friends continue to offer you* (241/15/61). (1390/49)

Grounding (55/1)

Plants grow towards the light because they need light to grow. It is exactly the same with each of us. Plant roots grow down because they need coolness and moisture. In the same way *each of us needs full contact with the ground* (110/20). (877/67/85)

Guilt (24/6)

Guilt is a sure sign that *your thinking is unnatural* (114/15/24). (226/28/46)

Light (The) (44/8)

An energy source always accompanied by *a deep feeling of peace and love* (123/15/33), sometimes overwhelming in its intensity. (497/47)

Light (The) (44/8)

To fully appreciate light, it is necessary to first experience and understand darkness (341/35/71). (385/25/34)

Love (18/9)

An affection of the mind caused by that which delights (229/49).

Love (18/9)

This should be experienced as an open clear emanation that wells up within the body-mind and projects through *the vortex of the heart* (99/18). (603/63)

Love (18/9)

Love without desires, craving, or attachment (173/11/83) is the key that vanquishes infatuation, enmity and delusion. You don't have to study a lot of scriptures, because *all ideas come from God* (87/6). It is not a question of knowledge but of love. (807/87)

Magic (24/6)

The science of the control of the secret forces of nature (245/29/65).

Magic (white) (53/8)

When *your spirit body* (83/2) and *your physical body* (87/6) are in the same time frame. Powerful people have presence. (563/23/59)

Meditation (47/2)

The act of observing yourself without thought (239/59).

Miracles (35/8)

Miracles arise from a miraculous state of mind or *a state of miracle readiness* (98/8). The miracle minimizes the need for time. *Miracles are selective in the sense that they are directed towards those who can use them for themselves* (389/29). (840/30)

Peace (21/3)

Mental and spiritual activity which is centred and controlled (266/23/86).

Perfection (self) (72/9)

Perfection is not static, it is dynamic. Not "I am what I am", but, "I am what I am becoming" (375/15/33).

Presence (real) (58/4)

Real presence only comes from people with aura, and *auras only exist around people who have succeeded in tapping the universal consciousness* (348/33/78). (562/22/58)

Remorse (39/3)

Remorse stems from the undistorted awareness that you have wilfully and unnecessarily acted in a hurtful manner, towards yourself or another person, that *violates your personal and ethical standards* (136/19/46). (781/61/79)

Restless (27/9)

Unresting, not resting, sleeping or relaxing: never still:

uneasily active: never ceasing: allowing no rest (458/44/98).

Right timing (71/8)

Relaxing in action. Timing and relaxing go hand-in-hand (311/32/41).

Sacrifice (46/1)

The destruction, surrender or foregoing of anything valued for the sake of anything else, especially, a higher consideration (112/13/22). (588/48/57)

Sadness (18/9)

Sadness is related to the opening of the heart (176/14/86). If you allow yourself to feel sad, especially if you can cry, you will find your heart opens more and you can feel more love. (677/47/65)

Salt (7)

The wisdom that comes with the bitter experience of life (238/22/58), especially *disappointment in the feeling realm* (158/14/68). (451/46/91)

Sexuality (39/3)

The centre around which revolves the whole of social life (100/10), as well as the inner life of the individual (149/59). (441/45/81)

Sexuality (39/3)

This is often challenged in *the midlife crisis* (87/6), *menopause* (37/1), *"one last fling"* (53/8). (335/38/65)

Sexuality (39/3)

It is not something limited to one part of the body. It permeates the whole of our being. It is *the vehicle for reaching out to others* (170/80), socializing, and perhaps becoming intimate with them. (819/99)

Sexuality (39/3)

Sexual contact involves much more than just having intercourse or releasing tension. It allows one to draw psychologically close to another person and share *the fullness of life* (77/5) within the loving embrace of *the sexual union* (62/8). (913/94)

Sexuality (39/3)

A romantic relationship soon becomes an addiction (198/18). As with a drug we want more of the thing that gets us high. The problem is that we get addicted to the person's form, not recognizing that it is *the energy we want* (78/6). We focus on the personality and the body and try to grab on to it to keep it. *By grabbing hold of the channel so tightly we are actually strangling it and closing off the very energy we seek* (455/41/95). (1816/97)

Sexuality (39/3)

Whenever there is *a tendency to repress one's sexuality* (140/50), one immediately becomes *improperly grounded* (111/12/21). Should this happen the likely casualty to follow will be either *one's body-mind* (60/6) or *one's spirituality* (81/9). (886/76/85)

Worry (38/2)

Worry causes one to have negative reactions to life that are completely antagonistic to one's deepest desires (456/42/96).

Willpower (52/7)

The power of the brain to override *wayward signals* (59/5) and reimpose normality (365/32/95).

Glossary B

Greater Understanding (98/8)

Cosmos (the) (36/9)
A universal science that seems to have all the answers (212/23/32).

Cosmos (the) (36/9)
The world or universe as an orderly systematic whole - opposite to chaos (336/39/66).

Horizon (the) (66/3)
The dividing line between heaven and earth (246/21/66).

Metaphysics (50/5)
The branch of philosophy which investigates the first principles of nature and thought (436/49/76).

Morphic fields (74/2)
Fields of information (102/12) which guide the development of a form of an organism, its behaviour, and even its mental functioning. (594/54)

Morphogenetic fields (104/14)
Invisible organizing factors which contain within them goals or future states towards which developing systems are moving. They are *wholistic organizing principles* (165/12/75). (830/20)

Mystical states (44/8)
Although so similar to *states of feeling* (64/1), mystical states seem to those who experience them to be also *states of knowledge* (66/3). They are *states of insight* (65/2) into *depths of truth* (63/9) unplumbed by the discursive intellect. They are *illuminations, revelations, full of significance and importance* (261/27/81). (1197/27)

Occult (the) (35/8)
Transcending the bounds of natural knowledge (170/80);

mysterious, supernatural, esoteric. (343/37/73)

Psyche (the) (48/3)

The soul, spirit, mind; *the principle of mental and emotional life* (178/16/88), conscious and unconscious (405/45).

Psychic (40/4)

That which is of the mind or psyche (193/13).

Psychology (59/5)

The science which studies the attributes and characteristics which certain living organisms possess by virtue of being conscious (570/39).

Religion (53/8)

An organized outward expression of belief that may or may not lead to *spirituality* (64/1). (389/29)

Spirit (37/1)

The essence of consciousness, the energy of the universe that creates all things (302/32). Each of us is a part of that spirit, *a divine energy* (77/5). So, *the spirit is the Higher Self* (138/12/48), *the eternal being that lies within us.* (146/11/56) (774/54/72)

Spirit (37/1)

Spirit always tends towards expansiveness, greater energy and aliveness (277/25/97). The form (ego/personality) tends towards what it perceives to be *safety, security and the status quo* (117/18/27), which is usually *a deadening experience* (105/15).

If you are able to observe yourself without rationalization you will begin to notice that when you trust yourself and follow your energy fuller, you feel better. (1595/65)

Spiritual experiences (104/14)

These happen only for the growth and benefit of the seeker, and they vary according to the needs of each individual (577/37/55).

Spiritual experiences (104/14)

Can a spiritual experience be confined within a particular form? Nature always takes its own course; winds blow, fires burn, the water flows, all in their own majestic ways. Just as *God has assumed countless forms in the outer universe (195/15), the inner experiences (93/3)* that he gives us are equally diverse. (1111/22)

Spirituality (64/1)

Your relationship with The Source (42/6). (220/40)

Spirituality (64/1)

A state of being or a description of openness to *non-material life* (73/1). (420/60)

State of self-realization (the) (111/12/21)

The goal of spiritual practice is reached (283/13/22).

The breakthrough (77/5)

There is a big effort directed towards growth, like a young plant that pushes its way upwards *into the light* (66/3). Breakthroughs are possible now. Some choices must be made as to how to use your talents, abilities, and strengths wisely. This is a time for work and effort (138/12/48). *Remember this rule: you get further by modesty, perseverance and adaptability, than by violence or force (344/38/74). Be like a tree which grows steadily without haste and without pause* (257/23/77). The total of your small efforts will be something great. (2315/56)

The conscious mind (74/2)

The conscious mind is programmed by one's parents and teachers. Sometimes they are often confused themselves (485/35/44).

The consciousness (64/1)

A force that so many people undervalue. They do not focus on *the inner awareness* (81/9) or use its real power, even in the most difficult *moments of crisis* (71/8). (624/66/84)

The consciousness (64/1)

Something which is intrinsically correlated with itself; it has *self-knowledge* (57/3). It follows that if meaning is connected to correlation, and consciousness has *self-correlation* (73/1), then consciousness becomes something with *intrinsic meaning (88 / 7). (1012 / 13)*

The consciousness (64/1)

The consciousness is activated in response to sense perception (241/25/61). This in turn activates memory, and gives rise to thoughts, feelings, intentions to act, etc., which unfold into further activities of consciousness. (874/64/82)

The core of the soul (78/6)

If one believes that *abundant good* is available to one, one will find abundant good (46/1) in every area of one's experience. (521/53/71)

The core of the soul (78/6)

The heart chakra (64/1), which is the core of the soul, defines one's personality. (431/44/71)

The easy way (44/8)

There is something about the easy way, no matter what the area of life, that does in fact seem to suck us into it with accelerating speed and sureness of grip, like quicksand (65/35/62).

The easy way (44/8)

When there is *no going forward* (83/2), *no direction* (63/9), life becomes a drifting compromise with whatever circumstance happens to be thrown up. The result can be *frightening boredom* (108/18), or *massive escapism* (56/2). (846/36/81)

The ego (33/6)

The little outer self (79/7), *the personality self or "mask"* (110/20) developed over the years. (327/39/57)

The ego (33/6)

Everyone and their ego has free choice as to which path they choose to go down - *the path of happiness* (89/8) or *the path of ill-health* (87/6). The trouble is that so many people are so blind that they cannot see around the corner. (877/67/85)

The ego (33/6)

Everyone born on earth has *a fallen nature* (49/4), *an ego problem* (60/6) that has caused all the trouble in our lives on the planet. It is *pure selfishness* (69/6) in all its forms: greed, pride, lust - you name it. When allowed to run riot, it commits all the sins of the world. (950/50)

The ego (33/6)

The enlightenment of the form (132/15/42) happens through a miraculous process. As the ego surrenders to *trusting the universe* (94/4), *the spirit penetrates every cell of the body transforming the darkness into light* (346/31/76). (851/41/86)

The human will (56/2)

The human will can be one of the most obstructive energies (220/40). A person can see "a right path" and then almost deliberately take the wrong one. This interferes with *the Divine Plan* (67/4). (738/18/72)

The intuition (65/2)

When you are willing to trust and follow your energy, it will lead you into relationships from which you have the most to learn (523/55/73). The stronger the attraction, the stronger the mirror. So, *the energy will always lead you to the most intense learning situation* (272/29/92). (1111/22)

The intuition (65/2)

Knowledge based upon insight or spiritual perception (224/26/44), rather than on reasoning. (408/48)

The intuition (65/2)

The intuition is always one hundred per cent correct, but it takes time to learn to hear it correctly. If you are willing to risk acting on what you believe to be true, and risk making mistakes, *you will learn very fast by paying attention to what works and what doesn't* (276/24/96). (1101/21)

The joy (29/2)

When a mind has only light, it knows only light (190/10). Its own radiance shines all around it, and extends out into the darkness of other minds, transforming them into majesty. (666/36/63)

The joy (29/2)

When you see beauty anywhere, it is a reflection of yourself (246/21/66). There are mirrors everywhere. *Whatever or whoever you have a connection with is a mirror for you, and the deeper the connection, the stronger the mirror* (542/56/92). (972/18/99)

The joy (29/2)

Nothing you see in the mirror is negative (192/12). *Everything should be viewed as a gift that will bring self-awareness* (267/124/87), for after all you are here to learn; for if you were already perfect, you wouldn't be here. (666/36/63)

The potential for success (93/3)

This depends on *the alignment of one's spiritual and physical goals* (198/18). (354/39/84)

The self (30/3)

The interactive field between two brain generators (259/79).

The shadow (40/4)

To reject *the shadow side of life* (94/4), to pass by with averted eyes, refusing our share of common sorrow while expecting our share of common joy, would cause *the unlived, rejected shadows* (108/18) to deepen in us as fear, including *our fear of death* (71/8). (907/97)

The soul (28/1)

A spirit, embodied or disembodied (173/11/83).

The unconscious (60/6)

An energy pipeline or cosmic string (230/50).

The unconscious (the unknown) (106/16)

Without relating to the unconscious, it is impossible to extend the boundaries of what is known, or to gain new consciousness (477/27/45). Once particular speculations have passed into *the sphere of knowledge* (104/14), they become redundant. But *the capacity to speculate through symbols, through the imagination, shifts its ground, extends its bounds, or atrophies* (470/20). Only a particular attitude of openness can liberate the individual from his personal confines and limitation. (1917/18)

The vertical experience (110/20)

Most people live horizontally (136/19/46) and only a few effect *the vertical type of life* (109/19). The vertical experience is for *the overcomer* (66/3), and forms a cross with *the horizontal, ordinary human experience* (204/24). (1030/13)

Touch (22/4)

Touch activates your cosmic energy (163/19/73).

Transformation (66/3)

The transformation in nature - the way everything changes into everything else, reflects *inner processes of growth within your inner psyche* (249/69). (926/26/98)

Transcendent episodes (85/4)

These focus on the need for change. Perhaps the unknown or unconscious need for change is to become like a child again, so as to be able to take part in life fully. (679/49)

Transcendent experiences (107/17)

These have the possibility to alter a person's values. *Values can become hardened or outdated* (134/17/44), and a change may come about only with a jolt. (548/53/98)

Universal cosmic consciousness (115/16/25)
The final stage of personal development (269/26/89).

Glossary C

The Health Scenario (82/1)

Healing (38/2)
The attuning of the atomic structure of the living cellular force to its *spiritual heritage* (90/9). (406/46)
Healing (38/2)
Curing the body (72/9) involves also healing *the affliction in the psyche* (127/19/37). Effectively this highlights the contrast between *the physical cure of the body* (124/16/34) and *the cure of the whole person* (122/14/32), involving the mind and the destiny, which might include *dying at the right time* (107/17). (1192/22)
Healing (Quantum) (64/1)
The faculty of inner awareness (120/30) promotes a drastic jump - *quantum leap* (42/6) - in the healing mechanism. (418/49/58)
Healing (Quantum) (64/1)
The ability of one mode of consciousness (the mind) to correct mistakes in another mode of consciousness (495/45).
Healing (Quantum) (64/1)
This moves away from high technology method toward the deepest core of *the mind/body system* (80/8). This is where healing begins. To go there and *learn to promote healing* (108/18), one must pass through all the cells, tissues, organs and body systems to arrive at *the junction point between mind and matter* (162/18/72), the point where consciousness actually starts to have an effect. (1458/54)

Healing (self) (53/8)

Achieved by maintaining an image of an optimal body condition (152/17/62).

Healing (self) (53/8)

This means *self-transformation* (81/9). Any illness, whether it be psychological or physical, will lead you on a journey of *self-exploration* (74/2) that will completely change your life from the inside out. (878/68/86)

Health (27/9)

A positive process (76/4), *a permanent testimony* (87/6), *a structure of order* (83/2), which sets a world of order moving. (423/45/63)

Health (27/9)

The practical manifestation of the interplay of all energy within the name at any given point in time (435/48/75).

Health (the mechanistic, monistic approach to) (181/19/91).

This centres on the physical body, with little or no attention to the mental, emotional, or spiritual aspects (593/53).

Health integration (87/6)

The body and consciousness working in union (300/30).

Ill health (42/6)

More subtle levels of meaning may exist alongside *the physical aberration* (105/15), the ill health - levels that can shed light on *the disease process* (73/1), and transform it from something malevolent into something that can be seen *at higher levels* of understanding (142/16/52), possibly even as a positive event. (1140/24)

Ill health (42/6)

The fading sense of health (103/13) is perhaps because we have lost touch with *the imaginal realm of illness* (115/16/25). We seem to experience less and less *a sense of health* (57/3) when, technology assures us, we should be experiencing more and more. (883/73/82)

Ill health (42/6)

There are no victims, only volunteers (195/15).

Ill health (42/6)

Sickness or illness can have the effect of taking a person out of a problem, and thus they avoid making the necessary life change (106/16). (628/61/88)

Illness (27/9)

Though certainly not a dream in the ordinary sense, it may be described in a sense as a daydream, *a dream of the unconscious self* (111/12/21) which directs organic as well as psychic processes, and shapes *the whole pattern of life* (108/18). (829/19)

Illness (27/9)

Can be seen simply as a message from the body which says *"wait a minute, something is wrong - you are ignoring something very important to you, you are not listening to your whole self"*. (532/55/82). What is it? (795/75)

Malignancy (47/2)

Malignancy may be caused by *a disturbance in the self-regulating mechanisms of the body* (238/22/58), these mechanisms being probably *electromagnetic* (69/6) in nature. (620/80)

The body (36/9)

There is no secret to having *a beautiful body* (56/2). Simply *trust yourself* (57/3) and follow your natural needs. Tune-in and honour your intuition. *Keep the energy moving* (109/19) by backing yourself up moment by moment. Most importantly, *love and nurture yourself now* (120/30). You are beautiful. (1075/13)

The body (36/9)

Speaking of *the true body form* (80/8), that form which all would be were the lifetime used from the beginning in *a totally loving way* (74/2). No hint of negativity, no hint of illness, could touch the figure of the form so used. (924/96)

The body (36/9)

The body image is the key to the symbolism of the body (211/22/31), *the relationship of the body and mind* (160/170), and so sometimes *the key to discovering meanings of illnesses* (181/19/91), *emotional needs that are being expressed in terms of illnesses* (240/60). (861/51/87)

The body (36/9)

Disease of the body (74/2) is an end product, a final stage of something much deeper. It originates above the physical plane. (487/37/46)

The body (36/9)

The indulgent man (68/5) is he who will go on satisfying his senses until *his body becomes useless* (84/3). In the end his *wornout body* (75/3) torments him and he begins to hate it. *The renunciant* (62/8) too wears out his body with his unnatural forms of austerity. He develops enmity towards the body and tortures it. (1321/43)

The brain (41/5)

The brain and its inherent capacity (the psyche) is a bridge between the genetic, vegetative and the cosmic physical world. (525/57/75)

The brain (41/5)

The conscious awareness (85/4): *the immense dormancy of the brain* (142/16/52): *the physiological template to contact the subconscious* (204/24). (552/12/57)

Glossary D

Health Details (52/7)

Acne (14/5)

Not accepting the self. *A dislike of the self* (76/4). (175/13/85)

Ageing problems (71/8)

Social beliefs (54/9), *old thinking* (60/6), and *a fear of being oneself.* (93/3) *A rejection of the now* (89/8).(377/17/35)

Allergies (43/7)

A lack of trust in the intuitive (116/17/26). *Repressed feelings* (87/6). (246/21/66)

Back pain (30/3)

A feeling that you have to support others (162/18/72). *A need to express and support your feelings* (173/11/83). *Lower back pain is often suppressed emotional sadness* (194/14). *Upper back pain is often suppressed anger* (165/12/75). (724/76/94)

Bad breath (34/7)

Anger and revenge thoughts (114/15/24) with experiences that back up. (263/29/83)

Bedwetting (46/1)

The fear of a parent (78/6). (124/16/34)

Blood problems (58/4)

A lack of joy (36/9) and circulation of ideas. (189/99)

Breathing problems (85/4)

A fear or refusal to take in life fully (144/18/54). *Not feeling the right to take up space or even to exist at times* (237/21/57). (466/16/43)

Bronchitis (54/0)

An inflamed family environment (138/12/48). (192/12)

Brain tumour (53/8)

Incorrect beliefs (82/1). *Stubborn* (30/3). *Refusing to change old patterns* (127/19/37). (292/22)

Breast problems (57/3)

An over-mothering, overprotection, and an overbearing attitude (263/29/83). (320/50)

Cancer (26/8)

The incarnation of hunger in the soul (161/17/71). (187/16/97)

Cancer (26/8)

A possible path to enlightenment (126/18/36). (152/17/62)

Cancer (26/8)

A longstanding resentment (99/9). *A deep hurt* (44/8). *A deep secret or grief eating away at the self* (174/12/84). (299/29)

Cell regeneration (82/1)

One becomes aware that cell regeneration has commenced once *the skin becomes clearer* (93/3), *the breath becomes sweeter* (100/10). *The odours of elimination begin to diminish* (199/19), *the eyes will sparkle* (81/9), and *the tongue becomes pale and clear* (116/17/26). Also *the voice takes on a subtle but detectable musical tone* (162/18/72), and *the emotions are much easier to control* (158/14/68). (1249/34)

Chills (27/9)

A desire to retreat and be left alone (128/11/38). (155/11/65)

Colds (17/8)

When the brain sends out a signal containing "an expectation of a cold", that is exactly what will eventuate (393/33).

Colitis (33)

Inflammation of the colon, the large intestine (221/23/41).

Compulsive eating (74/2)

Greed is known to be often *emotional deprivation* (102/12), but the mind may even be off-loading other problems onto the body. *A hunger for greatness, for fame* (132/15/42), can be communicated to the body via the unconscious, and it complies by eating without comprehending. (1061/17)

Conjunctivitis (62/8)

Anger and frustration (90/9) at what you are looking at in life. (280/10)

Congestion (49/4)

The accumulation of blood in any part of the body (236/29/56).

Coronary thrombosis (96/6)

Feeling alone and scared (93/3). *I am not good enough and I don't do enough* (164/11/74). (353/33)

Depression (52/7)

The most destructive aspect of depression is the way it paralyzes willpower (356/32/86).

Depression (52/7)

Depression has the psychological effect of lowering (depressing) the level of consciousness (380/20) and thereby allowing *unconscious content* (73/1) to break through. (664/34/61)

Diabetes (29/2)

The longing for what might have been (159/69). *A great need to control* (86/5). *No sweetness left in life* (94/4). (368/35/98)

Earache (32/5)

Not wanting to hear (78/6). Too much turmoil and parents often arguing. *Angry* (31/4). (314/35/44)

Eczema (26/8)

The result of an *emotional shock* (61/7). (143/17/53)

Epilepsy (46/1)

A sense of persecution (85/4). *The feeling of a great struggle* (129/39). *A rejection of life* (81/9). *An opportunity for self-violence* (147/12/57). (488/38/47)

Facial hives (50/5)

A rash resulting from *an inability to self-express adequately* (153/18/63). *A sign of frustration* (88/7). *Developing multiple sclerosis* (129/39). (429/69)

Fat (9)

Anger that is withheld or blocked (143/17/53).

Fatigue (33/6)

Resistance boredom and a lack of love for what one does (224/26/44).

Fatigue (33/6)

Often one of the first symptoms of ill-health - *rheumatoid arthritis* (101/11), or *multiple sclerosis* (74/2), for example. (457/43/97)

Frigidity (64/1)

Fear or a denial of pleasure. A belief that sex is bad. Or insensitive partners. (355/31/85)

Gas pains (32/5)

Gripping or fear. Undigested ideas (185/14/95).

Glandular problems (73/1)

The pituitary without energy, which is all blocked around the pelvis (361/37/91).

Heart attack (36/9)

When *a real heart attack* (55/1) occurs, rub and pinch the fifth or smallest finger, for the endings of *the heart meridian* (86/5) can be found there. When *the heart really stops* (87/6), use the fingers to pinch a point above the middle of the upper. lip (941/95)

Heart attack (36/9)

Squeezing all the joy out of the heart in favour of money and position (329/59).

Heart problems (62/8)

Long standing emotional problems (133/16/43). *A lack of joy* (36/9). *A hardening of the heart* (106/16). *A belief in strain and stress* (101/11). (438/42/78)

Hernia (37/1)

A ruptured relationship (108/18). *Strain and burdens* (66/3). *Incorrect creative expression* (143/17/53). (354/39/84)

Hyperventilation (89/8)

Fear and resisting change (196/16).

Insomnia (40/4)

Deliberate wakefulness (122/14/32).

Kidney problems (69/6)

Criticism, disappointment, and failure (162/18/72). *Reacting like a kid* (76/4). (307/37)

Loss of appetite (61/7)

Protecting the self and not trusting life (230/50).

Menopause problems (74/2)

A fear of no longer being wanted and of ageing (186/15/96). *Self-rejection* (60/6). (320/50)

Menstrual problems (70/7)

A rejection of one's femininity (138/12/48). *A belief that the genitals are sinful or dirty* (182/11/92). (390/30)

Menstrual tension (pre) (87/6)

Allowing confusion to reign by giving power to outside influences (293/23). *A rejection of the feminine principle* (178/16/88). (558/18/54)

Migraine headaches (85/4)

A dislike against being driven (124/16/34). *Sexual fears may be involved* (100/10). (309/39)

Multiple Sclerosis (74/2)

Mental hardness, hard-heartedness, iron will, inlexibility and fear (353/38/83).

Peptic ulcer (56/2)

A belief that you are not good enough (145/19/55). *Anxious to please* (61/7). (262/28/82)

Prostate problems (70/7)

Mental fears weaken the masculinity (129/39). *Sexual pressures and guilt* (94/4). *A belief in ageing* (79/7). (372/12/39)

Respiration (63/9)

This does not simply mean breathing. It is used to describe all the processes associated with *the release of energy within the body* (170/80). (555/15/51)

Rheumatoid arthritis (101/11)

Feeling very put upon (100/10). (201/21)

Saliva (19/10)

Saliva has the power as a natural healing water (148/13/58). (167/14/77)

Sciatica (29/2)

A fear of money and of the future (126/18/36). *Hypocritical* (69/6). (224/26/44)

Senility (43/7)

A return to the so-called safety of childhood (170/80). *Demanding care and attention* (109/19). A form of control of those around you. (472/22/49)

Shyness (30)

Shyness represents *a blockage in the throat chakra* (111/12/21) which governs *the thyroid gland* (82/1). (372/12/39)

Skin problems (54)

Anxiety and fear (68/5). *An old problem from the past* (106/16). *A feeling of being threatened* (127/19/37). (355/31/85)

Skin rashes (42/6)

A want to break out and take action (98/8). *What are you itching to do* (108/18). (248/23/68)

Sickness (27/9)

The expression of an emotional need (147/12/57). (174/12/84)

Sinus problems (56/2)

An irritation to one person, even someone close (249/69).

Snoring (42/6)

A stubborn refusal to let go of old patterns (147/12/57). (189/99)

Stiffness (36/9)

Rigidity - lumbago, arthritis, rheumatism (180/90). *Rigid mental attitudes of an over-masculine kind* (183/12/93). *The lack of feminine anima or feminine qualities* (208/28). (607/64)

Stress (19/1)

Any stress on the body leads to *a diminution of energy*

(115/16/25) in the specific meridian relating to unhappiness, *the liver meridian* (91/1). (547/52/97)

Stress (19/1)

Freedom from stress is obviously going to improve the brain's chances of reimposing corrective control over its cells (523/55/73).

Stroke (25/7)

A rejection of life (81/9). *Rather die than change* (97/6). (203/23)

Tension (33/6)

The sign of *accumulated tension* (65/2) is when one stands with one's feet in different directions. (388/28/37)

The arms (30/3)

These represent the capacity and ability to hold onto *the experiences of life* (110/20). (333/36/63)

The bladder meridian (89/8)

The predominant emotional states affecting *the energy balance* (75/3) are restlessness (39/3), *impatience* (50/5), and *frustration* (53/8). (500/50)

The breath (42/6)

The ability to take in life (105/15). (147/12/57)

The colon (38/2)

The garbage pail of the body and the seat of many illnesses (88/7).

The elbows (37/1)

Represent *changing directions* (98/8) and *accepting new experiences* (75/3). (220/40)

The feet (33 /6)

These represent one's understanding of oneself, of life, and of others (310/40).

The left shoulder (70/7)

This will often accommodate *a protective attitude towards the heart* (149/59) by rotating slightly forward in *a posture*

224

that suggests a guarding action (146/11/56). (603/63)

The liver (45/9)

The seat of anger and primitive emotions (169/79). (214/25/34)

The heart (40/4)

The centre of transformation (122/14/32) that enables universal energy to transform into spiritual, and earth energy to transform into healing. (577/37/55)

The heels (37/1)

A person with a tendency to stand on his heels is one with *a self-defensive problem* (96/6). (352/37/82)

The meridians (62/8)

These may be the threshold between *pure energy* (64/1) and its first manifestation as microscopic matter. (446/41/86)

The neck (30/3)

This represents *the ability to be flexible in one's thinking* (182/11/92), to see *the other side of a question* (116/17/26), and to see *the other person's viewpoint* (131/14/41). *A neck problem* (52/7) usually means that one is being stubborn about one's concept of a situation. (893/83)

The neck (30/3)

A stiff neck is unbending bullheadedness (145/19/55). (175/13/85)

The pancreas (47/2)

This is controlled by *the pituitary gland* (86/5) which is governed by *the sixth chakra* (65/2). (384/24/33)

The shoulders (55/1)

These are meant to carry joy, not burdens. How bent are your shoulders (316/37/46)?

The spine (42/6)

The flexible support of life (166/13/76).

The throat (43/7)

This represents *one's ability to speak up for oneself*

(138/12/48). When there is a problem, it usually means that one feels one does not have the right to do so, one feels inadequate to stand up for oneself. (748/28/73)

The throat chakra (67/4)

Blockages are *a resistance to the feeling of emotion* (154/19/55). Always have faith in what you are doing. (420/60)

The thymus gland (62/8)

This secretes a hormone called thymosin whose basic function is to alert the body's mechanism to attack by foreign organisms (561/21/57).

The thyroid (62/8)

Never getting what you want to do (128/11/38). The ensuing *thyroid energy deficiency* (145/19/55) will reduce the metabolic rate and may even cause bowel cancer. (602/62)

The toes (29/2)

These represent the minor details of the future (226/28/46).

The tongue (43/7)

The most deadly member of the human body is the tongue. We can kick with our feet and strike with our fists, but neither can do as much damage as *a loose tongue* (45/9). (606/66)

The voice (42/6)

The sound of the voice creates a subliminal impact. So many people have a voice like a hammer making all problems look like nails. Why are so many people so obnoxious (653/23/68)?

Varicose Veins (62/8)

Standing in a situation you hate (119/29). *Discouragement* (64/1). Feeling overworked and overburdened. (425/47/65)

Vision problems (71/8)

Not wanting to look at certain things within yourself or within the world. Often there is a decision early in life not to look at *what you are seeing intuitively* (139/49). When *the inner vision is shutdown* (126/18/36), *the external vision is impaired* (143/17/53) as well. (929/29/92)

Bibliography

Jensen, Bernard *The Chemistry of Man*, Self Published

Hall, Dorothy *What's wrong with you?*, Thomas Nelson, Australia

Hay, Louise *You can heal your life*, Self Published

Diamon, John *Life Energy*, Harper and Row, Sydney

Dychtwald, Ken *Bodymind*, Pantheon Books, New York

Homan, Frank *Kofutu Touch Healing*, Sunlight Publishing, Philadelphia

MacLaine, Shirley *Going Within*,

Avery, Kevin Quinn *The Numbers of Life*, Dolphin Books, New York

Clay, A J Mackenzie *The Numbers of Health*, Self Published

Phillips, Dr David A. *The Secrets of the Inner Self*, Angus & Robertson

Index